Spirit and Light

SPIRIT AND LIGHT

Essays in Historical Theology

EDITED BY

Madeleine L'Engle

AND

William B. Green

A CROSSROAD BOOK

The Seabury Press • *New York*

The Seabury Press
815 Second Avenue
New York, N.Y. 10017

Printed in the United States of America

Library of Congress Cataloging in Publication Data

Main entry under title:
Spirit and light.
"Crossroad books."
1. Theology—Addresses, essays, lectures. 2. West, Edward N. I. L'Engle,
Madeleine. II. Green, William B., 1927–
BR50.S67   230   76–17834   ISBN 0–8164–0310–4

In honor of Edward Nason West

Contents

Foreword

The Rt. Rev. Horace W. B. Donegan
XII BISHOP OF NEW YORK

IT IS a special pleasure for me to write the foreword of this volume of essays in honor of Edward West, who throughout my episcopate of twenty-five years in the Diocese of New York served as sacrist, canon, and in the latter years, subdean of the cathedral, and who for all these many years has been my colleague and friend.

Others will write of his extraordinary career and accomplishments, of his wide and vast knowledge and of his talents in the varied field of the fine arts. As his bishop and chief pastor for more than a quarter of a century, it has been a joy to me that my predecessors had the wisdom to seek him out, and that their trust in him was not only not mislaid, but that he exceeded what must have been their fondest hopes. Canon West found a unique and enduring place for himself at the cathedral, which time has proven was made for him. It gave him an unusual opportunity for the exercise and development of his manifold natural abilities, and not only enriched the total life and work of the Cathedral Church but, one rejoices to believe, has brought to him the deepest joy in his ministry and priesthood. And when this happens for any priest, it brings nothing but joy to the heart of his bishop.

On the occasion of Canon West's thirtieth anniversary as a member of the cathedral staff, and later its chapter, at a memorable service when the Mother Church of the diocese was crowded with those who gladly came to do him honor, I expressed to him and to the vast congregation assembled there my personal appreciation and my recognition of his loyal, able and devoted service to his bishop, to the cathedral, to the diocese and to the Church at large. At this time I would only wish to reiterate strongly what I have made plain to all in the past.

I am glad that discerning friends have conspired and cooperated to offer to Canon West this volume of essays in his honor. He richly deserves this grateful testimony, and it gives me great happiness to share in it and to extend to him my best wishes and my blessing for the days and years to come.

Spirit and Light

I

Canon West of the Cathedral

   *Leslie J. A. Lang*

CANON WEST of the Cathedral. Many call him Edward, a
few Eddie, many more Ed, but to a multitude whom no man
can number, for decades now and across the country and
throughout the world he is known, admired and respected as
Canon West of the Cathedral. It is a fact, and not a boast that
the cathedral is the Cathedral Church of St. John the Divine
in New York City.

Bishops have come and gone; deans have moved onwards
and upwards, some spiraling into episcopal orbit. But the constant factor, since what now seems time immemorial, has been
this intriguing canon, who is called Father and Mr. Sub-dean,
and Professor and several kinds of Doctor. Even if he were to
become an archbishop his most familiar title would be everlasting.

This introductory chapter, through which the author is per-
mitted to keep company with distinguished friends of the
Canon who pay him honor and homage, cannot be a definitive
biography. Time must pass, and the pen of a more ready

writer appear for that. The difficulties and dangers of writing about a living person are obvious. If *de mortuis nihil nisi bonum,* so indeed of the living. In case anybody should imagine that time would bring forth startling revelations concerning the subject of this brief essay, let it be said that those of us who have known him for many, many years know nothing and have heard nothing but good. To speak the truth, or as much as anybody has the right to know, without embroidering it, without canonizing the subject or descending to flattery, is in this case not too difficult. For the truth about Edward West is substantial, intriguing and eminently worthy to be spoken. And it is the truth about a very private person, who does not wear his heart on his sleeve, speaks little about himself and has been entirely objective in his proclamation of the Word of God, in the exercise of his priesthood and in the creation and manifestation of beauty of word, color, form and design.

Edward Nason West had the great and good fortune to be born in Boston, to be born on November 5, 1909 and to be born of Edward Nason West and Isadora Angelina d'E. Bellizia. He was a child of New England out of old England and of that civilization of warmth and beauty of southern Europe. No wonder we see in him steadiness, application, dependability, competence to deal with hard facts and the realities of life. These qualities are joined to finesse, flamboyance and a "fine Italian hand," which can paint, carve, put pleasing and noble words together and, at the same time, discover, elicit and inspire the talents of others.

The home of the Wests was a happy one, the son devoted to his parents and the parents delighting in the son who at a very early age must have shown the promise of the future. A friend and contemporary of Edward's Boston University days has verified that and has added the charming fact that Edward was known to have escorted some of the most beautiful and engaging young ladies of the city. A dear and close friend of Cathedral days, upon hearing this, exclaimed, "I can well believe it!"

From the distant past has come the rumor that one of Edward's godparents was an ambassador to Russia, and so there and then began the third strand of cultural and spiritual influence to be added to his natural inheritance. It is not surprising that at the moment of this writing, a stranger might well conclude that at the Cathedral there is a patriarch in residence. When announcing Edward's forthcoming visit to preach at the Service of Carols and Procession at Epiphany, the rector of an illustrious midtown Manhattan parish, stated, "You must come and hear him and see him, for he not only speaks, but he *looks* like a Wise Man from the East." Behind the patriarchal appearance lies a spiritual kinship with the Orthodox Churches of the East, a deep and abiding friendship with the saints and leaders of those Churches throughout the world, an incredible knowledge of their liturgies and love for their art and culture.

Ecclesiastical Boston in the days of Edward West's youth was in the afterglow of the famous preaching, the rich ministry, and the brief episcopate of Phillips Brooks, a majestic and ecumenical figure whose sermons, evangelical, powerful and persuasive, moved the hearts and minds and wills of multitudes. Many able and dedicated young men, under the spell of Brooks, came to the Episcopal Theological School from everywhere, and many remained in Massachusetts after ordination. William Lawrence, the dean of the school, had succeeded Brooks as bishop of the diocese, and under his leadership it attained a greatness, solidity and strength which remain to this day.

These were the days before the trek to the suburbs had begun. The churches of Boston were numerous and full, and especially the Episcopal churches. Ancient St. Paul's Church had become a cathedral and a strong center of diocesan activities and worship, suitable to the needs of the diocese and the times. Henry Sherrill, later to become the Bishop of Massachusetts, had led Phillips Brooks' Trinity Church into renewed strength and vigor. Dr. Elwood Worcester, rector of Emmanuel, had become the precursor with his Emmanuel

Movement, in the whole field of spiritual healing, which we all so take for granted today.

Notable among the city churches, and second to none in power and influence, was the Church of the Advent at Brimmer and Mount Vernon Streets at the foot of Beacon Hill. Here was to be found catholic worship in glory, taste and splendor, which together with the remarkable preaching of Dr. William Harmon Van Allen, its rector, more than taxed the capacity of the church. It was to the Advent that Edward West made his way and became a part of its life, and what is of equal importance, the church became an enduring and permanent part of his life.

Father Van Allen was a unique and famous personality. His untimely death in 1931, the year Edward went to seminary, made the front pages of the national press. One does well to dwell on his career, for reasons which will become obvious. The rector attracted to the Advent not only the rich and the great (in fact, they had always been there), but leaders in the social, intellectual and cultural life of greater Boston. He was a tireless worker for religion in its broadest interests, and his friends were of all creeds and classes. He was a member of innumerable organizations for the welfare of mankind. With power and courage he faced the issues involved in World War I, capital punishment, prison reform, child labor and local civic affairs. During the war he went to Europe to preach the Gospel, bringing courage and encouragement under fire. It should be noted at this point that during World War II, through the canon's instrumentality, a quiet work of rescue of the oppressed of Europe went on at Morningside Heights. He was honored by foreign governments and our own. He filled the Advent with beauty of sound and color— the magnificent hanging rood, the glorious Kirchmayer carvings, the clerestory windows—all of which enhanced the dignity and fine lines of an enchanting building. What a rector of the Advent Edward would have made!

Out of this background of Boston and the Advent, Edward

came to the General Theological Seminary at Chelsea Square in New York City in 1931. One recalls a tall, dignified, pleasant, extremely presentable young man, more slender than now, with a fine head, an abundance of dark hair, a trim mustache and entirely unprovincial speech. He did his work quietly and well, learned what he came to seminary to acquire; we liked him and he liked us. Many of us had known richer liturgical fare than was then current at General, but the historic faith was taught and commended, and every opportunity was afforded to practice it. The simplicity of life and worship was good discipline for everybody, and the grace and beauty of what might well have been an Oxford college transplanted to New York, an oasis between an elevated railroad and a freight train line, remains a part of one's life. It was one of the golden ages in the Seminary's long history, perhaps with as unique a faculty as was ever gathered together in one seminary at one time. Any of Edward's contemporaries who may read these lines will recall the names of Hughell Fosbroke, the dean for thirty fruitful years, Frank Gavin, Leonard Hodgson, Burton Scott Easton, Marshall Bowyer Stewart, and last but far from least, Cuthbert Simpson, each eminent and preeminent in his respective field.

Edward has remained a friend of General for forty-five years. Honored by it, he brought beautiful things to it, and taught its students for a long time.

Edward was ordered deacon in 1934, and ordained priest in 1935 by the Bishop of Massachusetts. Those were the days of the Great Depression, and Massachusetts, like so many of the great dioceses at that time, was overpopulated with priests. Parish budgets were slim. Hence some of us were accepted by the Diocese of New York. Undoubtedly the next best thing to being in Boston is to have come from Boston, and if that were to mean a lifetime spent in the Church in New York, then one was doubly blest. Life in this diocese is unusually happy and fulfilling for clergy and laity alike, because of the leadership of a distinguished succession of bishops. They have exercised pastoral care, compassion, social concern and have been faithful and untiring shepherds of the flock committed to their charge.

In 1934, Father West became curate of Trinity Church, Ossining, an attractive and substantial downtown edifice, with a cross section of the people of that rather famous Hudson River town. The rector of the parish at the time was Father William Gibson Harris. Advanced in years, he had enjoyed an enduring and faithful ministry there, and was a devoted pastor with a deep sense of our Anglican inheritance. The young assistant, to be advanced to the priesthood a year later, was the man for that hour and place. We used to call the curacy, in our ebullient, youthful days, "bringing up Father." At any rate, the respectful and competent curate established lasting friendships, and upon the death of the rector in 1937 was himself elected to that position. The vestry and congregation had had ample time to know what they were getting, and they were happy in their choice. His gifts of leadership, preaching and liturgical discernment were manifest from the start.

It must have been at this juncture that Edward began the life-long process of enriching and doing over church buildings. The Order of the Holy Cross was at the time going through a Benedictine phase, as its prime mover called it, removing lace frontlets, substituting full frontals, and otherwise simplifying the building. In the process, and quite rightly, the very handsome stone and statued reredos behind the main altar were removed from Ralph Adams Cram's French-Spanish country chapel. With the instinct and intuition which has characterized him to this day, Edward learned of it and found the right place for it—behind the high altar of Trinity Church.

It is always an interesting exercise, and surely a harmless one, to contemplate what would have happened had the chain of events been different. One has no doubt that a book would have been written and a tribute paid had Father West moved on from Ossining to any number of places, possibilities and responsibilities. However, in 1941, two astute men of perspicacity and vision, Bishop William Thomas Manning and Dean James Pernette De Wolfe saw fit to invite Edward to become Sacrist of the Cathedral Church of St. John the Divine.

One can surmise that their intent was to commit to responsible hands the liturgical round of prayer and praise, the innumerable occasions of special ecclesiastical, diocesan or civic significance, the great feast days of extraordinary splendor. The young sacrist was also entrusted with the care and preservation of the furnishings of the cathedral and its treasures, and direction of its future acquisitions and developments.

One can more fully appreciate the magnitude of the new sacrist's responsibilities if one realizes that these were the years before activism and programs, when, as stated in its articles of foundation, the Cathedral was to be a center of worship and learning and a house of prayer for all people. If this would seem to have limited either the use or the usefulness of the Cathedral, this was far from so. People went to church in those days and they went to the Cathedral's daily morning and afternoon services, in large numbers on Sunday mornings; in the afternoons (when often busloads might appear from a number of parishes in the diocese) and on high and holy days. On weekdays, one recalls the now unbelievable numbers, often more than filling the crossing, who came in successive weeks to the Diocesan Schools of Religion sponsored by the Dean and Chapter. So appealing were the lectures that evening sessions were called for in downtown churches, as a sort of cathedral extension, so that those who worked in the city might have an opportunity to hear the distinguished speakers. This was the Cathedral that people knew and used and had in mind. If one is nostalgic, one is also even more grateful, and this is not to denigrate those who bear responsibilities in changing times with changing patterns of life and devotion.

It is also important to bear in mind that in a "polychrome" diocese cathedral worship must be a mean between extremes, but it must also be faithful and true to our Catholic and Apostolic inheritance. The Eucharist had for some years been established as the chief act of worship on Sundays, with linen vestments and strict Prayer Book rite. This was not always pleasing to those with prejudices in either direction. Some Anglo-Catholics fussed because things were moving too slowly, and some Evangelicals carped because they were moving at all. But in the main the worship commended itself to the diocese. One saw what could be done in parish churches with the tools at hand. One could worship at the Cathedral and return home with some hopes of emulating what one had heard and seen. By steady, persistent, intelligent procedure, the Cathedral had become a chief influence in enriching the liturgical practice of the whole diocese. Canon West has had an incalculable part in all of this, acting with the permission, encouragement and approval of those in authority over him.

Circumstances conspired happily for the young sacrist—he was then thirty-two years old—to begin his association with the Cathedral in a burst of glory. For in 1941 the wall between the nave and the crossing was removed, and the Cathedral stood open before our eyes from Amsterdam Avenue to Morningside Drive, the longest ecclesiastical vista in all of Gothic Christendom. A serious conversation took place at the time as to what to call the service in celebration of the event. Bishop Manning and the sacrist decided that since the Cathedral had never been closed, it couldn't be called a reopening, and so the title appeared on the service leaflet "The Opening to Full View of the Cathedral." One wishes that truth could always be spoken so directly and simply in the Episcopal Church. Many of our parishes omitted the late morning service; the highways and byways were filled with church people on their way to Cathedral Heights. There were over sixteen thousand people in the building, some standing on the small flat protrusions on the pillars and in every conceivable place.

In 1943 the sacrist became a Canon Residentiary, and in 1966 he was appointed Sub-Dean.

How does one assess and appraise these thirty-five years of

devotion to a great institution? Quite simply, one cannot think of St. John's Cathedral without this particular canon. There have been most worthy and illustrious deans. They have come to earthly and heavenly rewards. There have been distinguished and dedicated bishops, but they could not always be present at the Cathedral. There has been a learned and goodly company of canons, some of them still with us. But Edward has become the very personification of the Cathedral, a canon par excellence. One pictures the tens of thousands of acts of worship, the visitations of royalty and princes of many Churches, the great occasions of joy and sorrow, the tremendous ecumenical gatherings, the Christmases and Easters, and everything carried out with dignity, grace, precision, tact and concern for the least among the greatest, with room for everybody and everybody in his place.

If all of this were not sufficient for one man, there has been the care and security of the Cathedral treasures and ornaments, of the seven chapels surrounding the the choir and the side altars and ornaments. It has been a constant source of joyous and frivolous but non-malicious merriment in clerical circles that anything movable in the building has not only been moved, but sometimes moved and moved again. There has also been a great succession of magnificent, sometimes startling additions. One thinks, for example, of the great crucifix now suspended before the choir at the west entrance, which some found to be grotesque in its original setting, and which now with its great strength and power seems completely appropriate. Canon West has made good use of what he found in the Cathedral when he arrived, displaying a number of things to greater advantage. He has been the agent of finding for the Cathedral numberless objects, good and beautiful. That everybody should be ecstatic about every detail is to ask more than can be demanded of humankind.

The methods employed by the canon to bring things new and old to the Cathedral are known only to him, but the author does recall that at the time the Mannings were moving from the former bishop's palace, Edward made frequent visits. On one occasion as Mrs. Manning saw him approaching, she said, "Canon West is on his way, and he's going to cast longing eyes on something else here for the Cathedral, and I am going to give it to him."

The canon is a skilled craftsman, with the heart and mind and hand of the artist and architect. What he cannot or does not do himself he has the ability to get others to do, enabling them to translate into wood and stone and precious metal what has already taken shape in his mind. Under his direction, ugly and nondescript church buildings have been made dignified and lovely. He sees in a moment exactly what can be done to reveal hidden beauty. He was able to assist the young rector of St. Peter's, Westchester, New York, to convince the vestry that the interior of a very fine 1850 French Gothic edifice, designed and built by Leopold Eidlitz, was hideously violated by peach-pink walls and red and yellow Navajo-rug patterns below the clerestory windows. White walls, preparing the way for later adornments to the building, revealed an exciting beauty which had theretofore been hidden. Time and time again this sort of thing has taken place with Edward's support.

To list the churches he has thus enhanced and to enumerate the prodigious works of beauty Edward has produced would require all the pages of this volume. But a few must be mentioned. There are the majestic Reigning Christ and matching candlesticks, in wood, at the high altar of the cathedral; the seven sanctuary lamps which hang before it, and the glorious frontals, made to be seen and appreciated by those sitting at the greatest distance from them; the great Iconostasis in the Serbian Cathedral of St. Sava (the former Trinity Chapel) on West 25th Street, Manhattan; the frontals and dorsals, the processional torches and the arrangement of the statues on the facade of St. Thomas Church; the delicately beautiful silver cross and candlesticks, made under his direction, for the communion table in ancient Trinity Church, Newport; the iconography of the more recent windows in the Cathedral; the

arrangement for the tomb and recumbent figure of Bishop
Manning; the emblem of the Anglican Congress; the chapels
for the Royal Navy, the American Merchant Marine and the
United States Military Academy at West Point. As one would
expect, the canon has long been the chairman of the Diocesan
Commission on Church Building, and vice-chairman of the
Joint Commission on Church Architecture and the Allied
Arts.

When in the course of human events the bishops of the
Episcopal Church ceased to be content to look like penguins,
or in court mourning, and became more happily arrayed in
red, Edward entered a new field of endeavor. He has designed
and redesigned red chimeres, and while the process has been
gradual, one suspects that the end product was long in the
creator's mind. At any rate, bishops now look better and
smarter and are more cheerful in appearance. How many of
them now possess copes and mitres and pectoral crosses and
rings and croziers by West! Each and every one of them is
distinct and beautiful and of special significance for the person
and his place. Of special note are the recently designed chalice,
paten and ciborium, incorporating the rings, pectoral crosses,
cufflinks and other jewelry of the late Bishop Stephen Bayne,
for his Cathedral Church of St. Mark, Seattle, Washington.

The story is told, and it is true, that a certain naughty but
most eminent priest once called the canon on the phone, and
in a disguised voice said, "Canon West, this is the Bishop of
. . . , and I want you to design me a coat of arms for my present
status." "Yes, indeed, Bishop, and do you have any special
ideas about it?" West replied. "Most certainly, I have. There
must be a bag of wind and a stuffed shirt. . . ." At that point
both burst into laughter, as the disguise evaporated. The worthy prelate, and he was that, has now long gone into the nearer
presence of the Lord—and he never was connected with the
Diocese of New York—and the eminent priest is alive and well
and, one is sure, will give no further information. It is more
important to serve bishops than to dress them, and no bishops

have ever been served more readily and faithfully than those in New York these past thirty-five years. They have deserved the service, and one is sure they have valued and appreciated it. As far as we know from Edward they have all been paragons of virtue, goodness, dedication and even temper, and Edward is a good judge of men!

The quietest and perhaps least well known interest and work of Canon West has been that of guide, mentor, spiritual director and Warden of the Community of the Holy Spirit. When Sister Ruth (now the Mother General) and Sister Edith Margaret visited England in 1949, they talked with several interested priests about the special vocation to which they felt called and for which they had the permission of their Canadian Community to explore. It was at this time that the name of Canon West was first mentioned to the sisters, who had already talked with Bishop Donegan in England. In due course the sisters discussed with the canon their vision of a House which would serve those coming to a new land and would itself have the witness and stability of Christian corporate living. The principal aspect of this vision could not be realized at the time, but not unrelated to it, the idea of a neighborhood school for young children came urgently to mind. Canon West was able to gather together a group of interested and committed people to share the sisters' hopes. The school is now over twenty-five years old, is housed in an impressive new building, and cares for some eight hundred pupils from nursery through high school

When in 1952 the sisters began the new Community of the Holy Spirit on Morningside Heights, prepared by Canon West for this momentous step, Bishop Donegan accepted the proposed Rule of Life and Constitution, and gave permission for the sisters to establish a Mother House in his diocese. Canon West was elected to the office of Warden in St. Columba's Chapel in the Cathedral directly after the election of the Mother on August 28th. He regularly celebrated the Holy Eucharist in a little room set apart as a chapel at the newly acquired St. Hilda's House, and with his own skilled hands provided the altar.

The Canon was responsible for training the new Community in the Sacrament of Penance, and for more than twenty years he has directed their spiritual life, conducted monthly retreats, and given the Community its long retreat every third year. He has been responsible with the Mother for the acceptance of Aspirants to test their vocations, has received each one of the Postulants into the Novitiate, and when preparation for vows for first and life Profession have been completed he has always presented the Sister-elect to the Episcopal Visitor.

The Reverend Mother General, who has kindly given almost word for word all of this information, has stated that the Community has looked to the Warden for guidance and counsel in every experience of its life. He studied the architects' drawings for the two schools, St. Hilda's and St. Hugh's in New York City, as well as for Melrose at Brewster, Connecticut and the convent there; he advised on all changes in the buildings as they affected the spiritual and religious life of the Sisters. He prepared the special liturgical services of blessings for the new houses and schools, as he did most recently when Archbishop Ramsey came to Melrose to bless the bells. He designed the sisters' crosses, and helped modify their habits so that they still look like Sisters, albeit in a modern world. The extent of all this can better be appreciated when one realizes that the Community of the Holy Spirit has been an unbelievably fast-growing order and is now among the largest and most active in the Episcopal Church.

In addition to his spiritual duties with the Community, the Canon has been a wise and sympathetic counselor and confessor to a multitude of people. He has encouraged many seekers in his frequent retreats and quiet days, and has been a cogent and persuasive preacher in the Cathedral for more than three decades, and in the cathedrals and great churches in England. Canon West has been Select Preacher to Trinity College, Dublin, has served as head of the Division of Christian Education in the Diocese of New York, Lecturer in Liturgics at the General Theological Seminary, Washburn Lecturer at the Episcopal Theological School, Lecturer on Education at New York University, Lecturer in Anglican Doctrine at Union Theological Seminary and Purser Shortt Lecturer at Trinity College, Dublin. He is currently Lecturer at the Cathedral's Institute of Theology and a member of the Commission for Anglican/Orthodox Doctrinal Discussions.

Although this homely essay cannot be systematic or exhaustive, and because time must pass before the long view can be taken to give a balanced and proportionate presentation, nevertheless one can try to be as complete as possible. Therefore, I offer some plain and unadorned facts as a matter of record, and they will speak for themselves.

Canon West has been honored from all quarters: He is Sub-Prelate of the Order of St. John of Jerusalem; Chevalier of the Legion of Honor of France; recipient of the Silver Medal of the Red Cross of Japan and State Conspicuous Service Cross; Officer of the Order of the British Empire; Officer of the Order of Orange, Nassau, the Netherlands; recipient of Archpriests' Crosses of the Russian Orthodox Church; Patriarchate of Jerusalem and the Serbian Orthodox Church; Commander of the Order of the Holy Sepulchre, Patriarchate of Jerusalem; Commander of the Order of St. Mark, Patriarchate of Alexandria; Order of St. Gregory the Illuminator, Patriarchate of All Armenians; recipient of the Cross of Lalibela, Patriarchate of Ethiopia.

Locally, he is Honorary Associate of the American Guild of Organists and for many years its chaplain; Chaplain (Major) of the 1st Battle Group, 107th Combat Arms Regiment; Chaplain (Major) of the 11th Internal Security Battalion, New York Guard. He has also served as Commissary to the Bishop of Polynesia and has three times been a delegate to the General Convention of the Episcopal Church.

Institutions of higher learning, here and abroad, have bestowed their honors on him: Litt.D. from Boston University where he earned his B.S. degree; S.T.D. from General Theological Seminary where he took his S.T.B.; D.D., Ripon College; F.T.C.L., Trinity College, London; Th.D., Institut de Théologie Orthodoxe, Paris; D.D., University of King's College, Halifax, Nova Scotia. Canon West is also a Fellow of the Royal Society of Arts.

Edward Nason West is the author of seven widely read and reread books: *Meditations on the Gospel of St. John; God's Image in Us; The Far Spent Night* (meditations for Advent); *Things I Always Thought I Knew; Byzantine Art* (a Monograph); *The Cathedral of St. John the Divine; History of the Cross,* the text for la Liberté's enchanting illustrations. He has contributed to the *Encyclopedia Americana,* Funk and Wagnall's *Universal Standard Dictionary, Living Thankfully* (four chapters) and *Confirmation: History, Doctrine and Practise.* In addition he was a consultant for "Theology and Anglicanism" for the *American Heritage Dictionaries.*

He serves as trustee of St. Vladimir's Orthodox Seminary and Academy, St. Hilda's and St. Hugh's School, the Society for the Promotion of Religion and Learning in the State of New York and the Tolstoi Foundation. He is a member of the Century, University and Columbia University Faculty Clubs of New York and the Athenaeum of London.

Edward West has a unique and abiding place among "the Men and Movements of the Episcopal Church." We pay tribute to a dedicated priest, confessor, director, preacher, scholar, artist, architect, ecumenist, writer and administrator. For many years at the Cathedral he has served intermittently and for long periods as Acting Dean. He has vast, deep and abundant knowledge. He is gracious, witty, amusing, a good companion and sincere friend, a lover of dogs and beloved of dogs. He has a goodly heritage as well as natural talents and endowments. He is a Renaissance man, both proud and humble who carries his honors well. To Canon West of the Cathedral, *ave* and *ad multos annos!*

2

The Mysterious Appearance
of Canon Tallis*

Madeleine L'Engle

THE CREATION of character is one of the most mysterious aspects of the novelist's craft. Where do the imaginary people who live, love, die, come from? Are they, in fact, imaginary?

The answer is paradoxical: no, they are not imaginary. They are real. They have lives of their own. Most novelists will agree that their characters are stubborn and willful; they do things which the writer never anticipated, and when character and writer have a clash of will, the writer would do well to listen to the character.

But if the character in fiction is real and not imaginary, that still does not answer the question of where Hamlet or Alice or Ivan Karamazov come from. To say that characters in a story think and act for themselves, that they are more alive than many of the people I talk with each day, is true; but it is not enough. They are real, for me, in a deeper sense of reality

---

*A small portion of this essay, in a different form, appears in *The Irrational Season* (Seabury, Lent, 1977).

than everyday relationships. But I don't bump into them on the street, as I may meet a friend. Where, then, do they come from? What is the writer's part in the creation of character? Antigone was not sent to Sophocles by God in a Machine. The depiction of character is not a magic act. How does the novelist exercise the craft?

Sinclair Lewis used to keep files on all his characters: color of eyes, hair, complexion; weight, distinctive features; church affiliation, clubs, etcetera.

I tried this once, but I found that it restricted the growth of my characters. I had tied them down so that they were not free to move. Of course, such a filing system insures consistency; a man who is skinny on page one isn't likely to become obese a hundred pages later; blue eyes will not turn brown. But if I do not know what my people look like without having to look them up, I do not know them well enough to write them. Or when, as sometimes happens, a character I thought of at first as being dark-haired and short should reveal himself, during the writing, to be, instead, fair and tall, if I have pinned him down on a file card, he isn't free to let me know what he really looks like.

Not that I don't take notes on the people who come to me to be realized; I do. I think about them for months, or years. I write about them on slips of paper which usually get lost. I describe them in my journal as they reveal new facets of character to me, or change in unexpected ways. Sometimes it is a long time before a character will name himself for me, and until I know someone by name I cannot write about him with any authority. A Stella will respond to a crisis differently from an Emily; a Matthew will not see things in the same way as a Simon.

Sometimes I will refer to these notes during the first draft of a book. More often, the fact of having written them down is enough to set the developing character firmly in my memory.

But where do these people come from in the first place?

The Mysterious Appearance of Canon Tallis

Doesn't the writer ever know? Occasionally. Not always. May
Sarton usually puts people she knows into her novels. Flan-
nery O'Conner saw the prototypes of her grotesque men and
women daily in rural Georgia. But only twice in my novels
have I been conscious of a character's source. I know exactly
where Rob Austin (who appears in *Meet the Austins, The Moon
by Night,* and *The Young Unicorns*) and Canon Tallis *(The Arm
of the Starfish, The Young Unicorns,* and *Dragons in the Waters)*
come from, and who they are in real life. I had no intention
of allowing either of them into my stories, but there they are,
like it or not, and there is not a thing for me to do about it
except to let them stay.

Rob Austin is one of my children, our youngest; Canon
Tallis is my confessor and friend. They have both taught me
that it takes far more technique, far more craft, to write from
a real person than an imaginary one. I must be true to the real
person, as far as my knowledge of that person and intuition
permits; and yet I must allow the character to develop inde-
pendently of the real person. This freedom may take the character into places and adventures the original will never know,
but it must not contradict the possibilities inherent in the
living person.

Is there any such thing as a completely imaginary character?
I doubt it. As the one to whom this essay is dedicated says, a
writer is a discoverer; he uncovers what is already there. Or,
he is an inventor; he takes inventory of what is already there.
He does not create *ex nihilo;* he uses this material in the most
concrete manner possible. For, as Henry James says, the job
of the novelist is to render, and not to report; to show not to
tell. And this rendering, this showing depends on all the people the writer has ever known; family, friends, people met in
airports, seen on buses or subways or on the street; all leave
their imprint on the subconscious, creative mind of the writer.
A character in a story may well be an amalgam of many people, some well known to the writer, some simply observed; and
the creative, below-the-surface mind will do the underwater

work and send the character up to the surface when needed. It is a mysterious act of collaboration between intellect and intuition.

When I was plotting *The Arm of the Starfish*, a novel of international intrigue, there was no Canon Tallis needed or anticipated. I had become fascinated by the strange fact that starfish and *homo sapiens* originally came from the same phylum; thus anything we can learn about the starfish is potentially important to our understanding of humankind. Thoughts of starfish, and what it would mean to our bodies if we could discover what makes the starfish capable of regenerating a lost arm, caused me to remember an article by Nancy Hale, read many years ago, about man's abandoned ability to cooperate with his own body; two thousand years ago, at the time when Jesus of Nazareth walked the earth, it was not uncommon for a person, especially a Holy One, to have amazing discipline of bodily functions: respiration, heartbeat, temperature. Such a person could also control heart, lungs, blood-pressure to such an extent that a physician would be unable to detect any sign of life. And such a Holy One could temporarily leave the body and move freely among the stars.

I'm not sure that all of this was in the article which I read in a magazine in a doctor's waiting room all those years ago; nevertheless the article had a profound effect on the original plotting of *The Arm of the Starfish*. Too many surgeons are knife-happy; we cut and mutilate when possibly we could heal. If body, mind and spirit were in collaboration instead of conflict, then we would not need our enormous, impersonal, overcrowded hospitals. When body, mind and spirit are separated, they are deprived of their potency.

Through my literary agent I was able to have the help of a marine biologist in setting up theoretical experiments with starfish, experiments consistent with what has already been done in research on the regeneration of tissue in starfish and other small animals. After this it was possible to take the known scientific facts and say: yes, but what next? What if . . . ? This process is called extrapolation, and the Yes, but what if . . . ? is implicit in all fiction.

When the research had been completed, I was ready to start the writing of the book. It was early summer and we were in our country home, Crosswicks, in the Litchfield Hills. One of my daughters and I were playing duets on the piano. We turned to a book of early baroque pieces and began playing a canon. One of our favorite family graces for many years was set to the melody of the Tallis canon, which we sang as a round, and while we were fumbling through the duet, the words reversed themselves for me, and Canon Tallis entered the plot of *The Arm of the Starfish*. He was still faceless, weightless, colorless. But the idea of a Canon Tallis filled me with mirth.

At that time I knew his prototype only as my confessor, someone immensely important to my spiritual well-being, someone who in his own marvelous way helped me to regenerate broken spiritual arms, but someone I had scarcely spoken to outside the chapel where I set before him and before God all the things which were troubling me. It certainly never occurred to me that it was he who would enflesh the imaginary Canon Tallis.

Early in the book, the young protagonist, Adam Eddington, was caught in a dense fog at JFK International Airport, and met a beautiful blonde young woman. Together they started to the coffee shop.

> Suddenly Kali stiffened and veered away.
> "What's the matter?" Adam asked.
> "I don't want him to see me."
> "Who?" Adam looked around stupidly and saw a middle-aged clergyman holding onto the hand of a gangly, redheaded girl about twelve years old.
> "Him. Canon Tallis. Don't look. Hurry."
> As Adam ran to catch up with her, she said, under her breath, but with great intensity, "Listen, Adam, please take this seriously. I'm warning you about him. Watch out for him . . ."

After this warning, Kali's plane was called.

Slowly he walked from the Alitalia gates to the Swissair waiting
room. There he saw Canon Tallis and the tall, gangly child . . .
standing with silent concentration licking ice cream cones, side by
side, each bowed seriously over the ice cream.
    Adam studied the clergyman and the child surreptitiously. The
only extraordinary thing about Canon Tallis was the fact that he
was completely bald, even to having no eyebrows, and had the
look, somehow, of an extremely intelligent teddy bear.

On the plane Adam watched the priest.

Across the aisle the canon and the child were eagerly peering out
the window, the priest leaning over the child, his arm around her.
He seemed very avuncular and not in the least sinister, and for a
moment Adam wondered if he could have dreamed Kali and her
warnings.

This brief discription was, for me, also a discription and an
unexpected one, of Edward West. At that time he did not sport
his magnificent beard, and while he did have eyebrows, removing them was taking the baldness of his hairless head one step
further. I had not yet seen him with a child, but subsequently
with my children he revealed himself to be just as avuncular
as he was with Poly. Instinct had guided me well.
    Adam's plane could not land in Lisbon because of the perva-
sive fog, and was rerouted to Madrid, where the passengers
were to be given visas. Adam's passport for some mysterious
reason did not satisfy the customs inspector who

led him into a bare room painted dark, oppressive grey. There was
an unshaded light glaring from the ceiling, a desk with a chair
before and behind. The one small, high window was barred.

The inspector proceeded to grill Adam in a harsh, accusing
manner. The young man began to think he was going to be
thrust into prison, when

The door opened and in came one of the uniformed men, followed
by Canon Tallis, looking grim.
    Adam suddenly remembered with horror all Kali's warnings.

He realized that they had seemed part of an adventure that was somehow make-believe; he had not taken them very seriously.
He took them seriously now.

Adam was halfway through his adventures and misadventures before he was certain that Tallis was not an enemy.

This ambiguity is not inconsistent with reality. The wider and deeper the personality, the more likely is there to be conflict and contradiction. A purely predictable character is easier to write, because such a character can be manipulated by the writer.

If I thought overmuch about the enormity of what I am attempting when I sit down at the typewriter to set down even the smallest work of fiction, I would not likely have the courage to continue, to be so rash as to bring characters like Tallis to life on the printed page. Fortunately I usually am well into a book before I realize what an audacious thing I am attempting; it seems to have crept up on me without my realizing it; and this is because a book of fiction, like the characters within it, has a life of its own.

I realize now, from hindsight, that the spiritual adventures into which I was plunging in *The Arm of the Starfish,* with the firm comfort and direction of my confessor, were just as wild as any outward adventures Adam might encounter. The analogy was far more direct than I realized during the writing of this novel.

With each book I write I become ever more convinced that each work of art, be it a great masterpiece or something very small, has its own identity, and it comes to the artist, be he genius or tiny talent, and says, "Here I am. Write me." Or, "Paint me." Or, "Compose me."

Several years ago I saw a short play written by a student at General Theological Seminary, in which an unborn soul is choosing its prospective parents. This is more or less what a book does with me (though sometimes I question why it would make such a choice). It comes to me and says: "Here I am. Give birth to me. Enflesh me."

The willingness to accept this extraordinary invitation, to be the bearer, the birthgiver of the work is an affirmation of Incarnation, and the fearfulness of this responsibility may be part of the reason why many people look down on fiction (or painting, or composing) with both condescension and uneasiness. When my mother was a child, no one in that good Episcopal family was allowed to read fiction on Sunday or to sing anything except hymns. Fortunately, nothing in the Bible was considered storytelling, and the children would hide in a big closet and read all the "dirty" parts, which had been deleted from the day's selections. Story has come to be so misunderstood and so distorted that I was once accused, when I was in an English boarding school, of "storytelling," when, in fact, the accusation was the deadly serious and unjust one that I had told a lie.

Story, poetry, music, painting are distrusted because they are supposed not to be real. They are supposed not to be true. But people both before and after Pontius Pilate have had good cause to ask, What is truth?

Once when I suggested to a student that he go to the encyclopedia when he wanted to look up a fact, he asked me, "But can't I find truth in stories, too?" I replied, "Who said anything about truth? I told you to look up *facts* in the encyclopedia. When you're looking for truth, then look in art, in stories, songs, sculpture."

This student was making the same mistake as many of his elders, confusing provable fact with truth; and then fearing truth enough to try to discount it. If I want to search for the truth of the human heart I am more apt to go to Dostoevsky's *The Brothers Karamazov* than a book of anatomy. But, it is said, *The Brothers Karamazov* is storytelling; it's fiction, and fiction isn't true, so it doesn't count.

At this moment in time, there are still denominational colleges which have splendid mathematics or history departments, but which do not permit theater departments because to act, to play the role of another person is a lie; and so an indispensable vehicle of truth is rejected.

I have been married to an actor for thirty years, and have learned that this trying on, this delving deep into roles is not only one way of finding out who, in fact, we are; it is also a way of enlarging and deepening this who we are. An old actor told me a good many years ago that when there is an accident, the actor is temperamentally forced to go and offer his help, because his training has put him into the habit of putting himself in another's place. When he sees an old woman fall on the sidewalk, he *is* that old woman, in a conditioned reflex of self-abandonment, and so he cannot hold back from helping.

I wish this were true of more people. It ought to be, and it certainly was of the person who told it to me. And it ought, of course, to hold true for the writer. The terrifying, audacious, exciting job of creating character both enlarges and deepens my own self and my understanding of and compassion for all people. At its most powerful, it frees me from the shackles of self-centeredness into the freedom of self-abandonment. Where I see in my neighbor not so much myself as the Christ, so in the parable of the Good Samaritan, the Christ figure is not the Samaritan, but the man set upon by thieves.

But the telling of story is still considered by many a suspicious and frivolous activity.

A young woman told me recently that she had been asked by an acquaintance what she did. When she replied that she writes poetry, the inquirer said, "Oh, I don't mean your hobby. . . ." And a friend, probing about how much a year I make in royalties, remarked, "And to think, most people would have to work so hard for that."

Make no mistake about it, a work of art, great or small, is work. It is hard work. El Greco's *St. Francis Talking with St. Andrew* did not spring full blown to the canvas. It encourages me to think of the enormous amount of rewriting Dostoevsky did—and many of the other writers I look up to as giants.

A book may come to me and ask to be written, but even the most minor of stories takes time and energy and considerable pain. But what joy there is, what surprise in attempting to serve the work. In this day when even professed Christians consider servanthood degrading, I deem it my greatest privilege to be allowed to try to serve the work which comes to me and demands my collaboration. Often I know that the work is asking me to go beyond my capacity. But once a story or a character or both have come to me, they will not let me alone until I set aside all objections and accept the challenge.

The acceptance of the challenge of service to the work is, again, an affirmation of Incarnation. God came to us as one of us, and he came as servant, not as opulent king or emperor. He turned the world's values upside down. What had heretofore been seen as great was suddenly seen as small. He confounded the wise and mighty with the foolish and the weak.

The Incarnation—Jesus as wholly man and wholly God— has always been the stumbling block to my understanding of Christianity. If Jesus is exactly like us, *except sinless,* then he is not like us at all. And how can the creator of the galaxies be contained in mortal flesh and bone?

The *how* I cannot understand at all, nor am I required to, and it is literature rather than formal theology which comes to the rescue of my understanding. No great character in literature is written in generalities. Generalities do not come alive, do not engage the reader. The greater the writer, the more particular the characters. Oedipus, Hamlet, Tess of the D'Urbervelles may represent the universal, but we understand the universal only through the particular; there is no other way. This is fundamental to human nature, and I am not at all sure that it is a limitation.

So if we are to understand anything at all: the power behind the stars; the meaning of our own lives; why God allows the innocent to suffer and the wicked to flourish, it must be through the particular, and the greatest particularity of all is Christ Jesus.

I cannot understand the Creator of the universe except as I understand him through his particular revelation, Jesus of

Nazareth. It wasn't miracles, during my dark periods of agnosticism, which kept me from the adoration of Christ. I've seen miracles; they're easy to accept. It wasn't even the sentimentalizing of Jesus in both art and theology; a reading of the gospels suffices to counteract this. No, it's the incredible idea that God could—would—come to us in this singular and particular way. Jesus is the ultimate particularity by which we understand everything else. He is the one completely free man who ever walked the earth. And that freedom led him to the cross. Perhaps this is why freedom is so difficult for us to accept.

Jesus is the protagonist of Creation, and this is a stumbling block for many of us, because we consistently make the mistake of casting ourselves in the leading role. The extraordinary thing is that Jesus himself never did this. Always he deferred to the Father; and this deference is a model of strength, not weakness.

The characteristic which makes it most possible for me to accept Jesus as God, and not just a nice rabbi, is that he never presumed to be the Father, never fell into the tragic flaw of *hubris*—usurping the prerogative of the gods. He was the one man who did not consider equality with God a thing to be grasped, but rather emptied himself, and so, was God.

This is what the story of the temptation is all about. Satan offered Jesus total worldly success: Show yourself as God now. You can, you know. Turn these stones into bread and feed all the poor, since your Father doesn't seem able to do so. Jump from this great height and call on your Father's angels to hold you up, and you'll win the whole world with this display of your miraculous powers. Worship me, because I am the reigning Prince of this world. Forsake your heavenly Father and I will give you dominion over the world, right now.

But Jesus refused the temptation of hubris, pride, being a Dictator God. How often we wish he had not rejected Satan's proposal! There would be no more diseased and starving children in India or South America or in our own slums. A few flashy miracles would help us toe the line. If we were not preoccupied with Our Father's Kingdom, we might have law and order in our streets now.

Thus Satan daily continues his subtle wiles and tries to force us into thinking that Jesus really wasn't interested in the poor and hungry at all, and all he cared about was pie in the sky by and by.

Human beings throughout history have continued to fall for this idea of a dictator God who will legislate our lives and program our happiness. Hitler's great and evil power came about because he succumbed to each of Satan's temptations, and was encouraged to do so by a desperate populace who wanted bread in their kitchens and immediate law and order in their streets.

The tragic hero is a man who might have rejected the temptations but did not. The witches tempt Macbeth in the beginning of the play by telling him that he is going to be king; they have knowledge of the future. Of course, Macbeth wants to be king. But Duncan is on the throne. Yes, but Macbeth would be a better king. From this it is a short step to the murder of Duncan and the eventual, inevitable fall of Macbeth. For the tragic hero always falls, reenacting mythically the prototypical tale of Adam and Eve.

While Shakespeare was, in his blood and bone, a Christian, all art is an affirmation of Incarnation, whether this affirmation is conscious or unconscious. The artist has been given, like it or not, the painful gift of perceiving reality more acutely than other people.

C.S. Lewis, leaving the hospital where he had been told of Charles Williams' unexpected death, found that the familiar streets he walked through were strange and new, painfully perceived as though for the first time. The same change of vision was true for his friends; the whole world seemed transfigured.

I was in early adolescence when my maternal grandmother died. We were spending the summer with her at the beach, and her death, too, was unexpected. I was the one who was with her when she died and who had to go in to my parents in the dark hours of the early morning, well before dawn, wake them and say, "Please go in to Dearma," as all her grandchildren called her.

We had to drive into town. I remember my sense of shock as we drove through the crowded streets of midtown that everything wasn't physically different, that everybody didn't know that Dearma had died. The world was irrevocably altered, yet nobody we passed on the streets knew it, and this seemed to me outrageous.

This was more than a selfish, childish reaction. I think that perhaps we are supposed to walk more often through the streets of that different world, where all our awareness is more acute, not our awareness of ourselves or our own subjective reactions, but an awareness that we are part of each other, that no man is an island and that separation from one another is not freedom, but death.

For me the meeting of these two worlds, the world in which we move and do our daily chores, and the transcendent world which an experience like Charles Williams' or my grandmother's death reveals to us, is in art. Now I confess that it is difficult for me to separate art and religion, for art is often the most authentic expression of religion. Confusion arises because some of the worst art, and some of the worst religion, is found in so-called religious painting or music or poetry. What I used to call Blood-of the-Lamb-ey hymns hindered me for a number of years from coming back to church. Pictures of Jesus as a pale consumptive, wandering along the shore of the Galilean sea, clutching his bleeding heart as he looks sorry for himself, have done immeasurable harm to both religion and art.

I also believe profoundly that the artist does not have to be consciously religious in order to produce great religious art. Sometimes—and this is hard for the overtly religious to accept —the atheist is better qualified to paint or compose or write for the church than the believer; not because he is an atheist, but because he has not been seduced by an idolatrous image of God. Therefore, it is easier for the Spirit to speak through him than through someone who sees God in his own image, controlled and tamed.

The depths of the artist's mind, no matter how atheistic the surface, is religious. To paint a picture or make music or tell a story is a religious activity. Timothy Kallistos Ware points out that an abstract composition by Kandinsky, or Van Gogh's landscape of the cornfield with birds, "is a real instance of divine transfiguration, in which we see matter rendered spiritual and entering into the glorious liberty of the children of God." And this, Ware reminds us, "remains true even when the artist does not personally believe in God. Provided he is an artist of integrity, he is a genuine servant of the glory which he does not recognize, and unknown to himself there is something divine about his work." And, Fr. Ware concluded, "we may rest confident that at the last judgment the angels will produce these works of art as testimony on behalf of the artists."

Montaigne says "the work of its own force and fortune can second the worker and surpass him, beyond his own invention and knowledge." An early example of this for me came shortly after I got out of college and was living in Greenwich Village in New York with three other girls. One of them has gone on to be a concert pianist. No matter what the rest of us were doing she practiced eight hours a day, finger exercises, one tiny phrase over and over again for what seemed forever. She was working on her first New York concert, and I'll never forget Handel's *Harmonious Blacksmith Variations,* or the Brahms *Second Piano Concerto,* or the Bach *Chromatic Fantasy and Fugue* as they slowly moved to life as she grew with them. If she diligently practiced the music, it also practiced her, and I witnessed the truth of Montaigne's words as I saw the great compositions pushing the young musician.

I learned something of "the force of the work" myself

shortly thereafter when I went through my first shattering experience of falling in love and having the love turn to ashes. I not only survived, but learned a great deal about the human heart through the writing of my first novel. As my protagonist deepened, so did I. This character was, at first, no more than a thinly disguised self-image. But as I learned, during the writing, to listen to the work, Katherine began to have her own separate identity. The more real she became, the more apart from me, the more I learned—both about the writing of fiction, and about myself. I learned, with this first novel, that it was not I who created character; it was character who created me.

When I was working on that first novel, I was genuinely and painfully unhappy. But while I was actually writing, I moved into a realm on the other side of unhappiness and was at play. Like a small child building a sandcastle, I was completely thrown into the activity, so that what might have been a totally destructive experience became, instead, a creative and freeing one.

I was freed by that time of writing as my book wrote me, not as I wrote it. The same thing holds true when I read a book; the books which matter to me are those which take over and read me. The music I play or listen to is that which actively participates with me in harmony and counterpoint. This is also true in graphic art. There must be an amorous interaction between the work of art and the person who is opening himself to it. Any actor will tell you that the audience can make or break an evening in the theater; the audience collaborates, quite literally, with the actor, to make something which is greater than either alone. But this is true not only in actual performances of plays or concerts, but in our response to a statue of Praxiteles or a painting of Roualt or a poem of Blake.

It is no coincidence that Jesus taught almost entirely by telling stories. And the Sermon on the Mount is not a sermon in any sense that we understand a sermon today. It is, in fact, poetry, and speaks to us in that language where the mind is enabled to enter the heart.

In *The Gates of the Forest,* Elie Wiesel tells this story:

> When the great Rabbi Israel Baal Shem-Tov saw misfortune threatening the Jews, it was his custom to go into a certain part of the forest to meditate. There he would light a fire, say a special prayer, and the miracle would be accomplished and the misfortune averted.
>
> Later, when his disciple, the celebrated Magid of Mezritch, had occasion, for the same reason, to intercede with heaven, he would go to the same place in the forest and say: "Master of the Universe, listen. I do not know how to light the fire, but I am still able to say the prayer." And again the miracle would be accomplished.
>
> Still later, Rabbi Moshe-Leib of Sasev, in order to save his people once more, would go into the forest and say: "I do not know how to light the fire. I do not know the prayer. But I know the place and this must be sufficient." It was sufficient and the miracle was accomplished.
>
> Then it fell to Rabbi Israel of Rizhyn to overcome misfortune. Sitting in his armchair, his head in his hands, he spoke to God: "I am unable to light the fire and I do not know the prayer; I cannot even find the place in the forest. All I can do is to tell the story, and this must be sufficient." And it was sufficient.

And Wiesel concludes, *God made man because he loves stories.*

When I start to write a book it is as though I am unable to light the fire, and I do not know the prayer. I cannot find the place in the forest. I do not even remember the story. All I can do is try to tell it.

This telling of the story which we cannot quite remember often springs from the deep waters below the conscious mind. I had written many books before I began to articulate any of these ideas, and I might never have done so had I not begun to do a good bit of lecturing and teaching. People ask questions about writing, about the creation of character, of story. Even if my answer to the question is a rueful "I haven't the faintest idea," it causes me to think; and sometimes, perhaps days or weeks later, my creative, below-the-surface mind will throw up a response.

If we human creatures were not willful and arrogant and fallen, the collaboration of intellect and intuition would not be as rare as it is. One of the results of the primordial fall is a continually widening gap between intellect and intuition, between mind and heart; and this gap is so terrifying to many people that they refuse to admit that it exists. I heard one supposedly educated and intelligent man announce defensively that there was no such gap between his intellect and his intuition, and that his conscious mind was completely in control of his unconscious mind.

But I think that most of us are willing to admit that we haven't come much further than Paul of Tarsus who stated bluntly that the things he did not want to do were the very things he did, and the things which he did want to do were the very things he did not do.

Neither am I in control of my subconscious mind; and my conscious mind is only a small part of the whole person I am meant to be. The old iceberg analogy has been so overused that we forget that it can still be instructive: Our conscious minds are the small part of the iceberg which is above the surface of the water, and the larger part of the iceberg, hidden below the surface, is the subconscious mind.

A surface scanning of Freud leads us to believe that the underwater area of the human being is totally foul and murky, full of sexual perversions and murderous repressions. These are there, there's no denying that. But they are not all. The ocean may and does know death and decay and putrescence, but there is also incredibly beautiful life, and the decay itself may be transformed:

> Full fathom five thy father lies;
> Of his bones are coral made;
> Those are pearls that were his eyes;
> Nothing of him that doth fade

But doth suffer a sea-change
Into something rich and strange.

—SHAKESPEARE, *The Tempest*

Jung glimpsed the richness of the below-the-water mind. And I too have learned slowly that the intellect, when it does not collaborate with intuition, is not only a poor instrument, but sometimes a vicious one.

This is what intuition was telling me when I made the villain of *A Wrinkle in Time* a naked, disembodied brain. It was only after the book was published that my conscious mind came to understand that the brain, when it is not informed by the heart, is evil.

"Pray with the mind in the heart," Theophan the Recluse urged. "Write with the mind in the heart" comes to the same thing, because storytelling (or painting, or composing a fugue) is a form of prayer.

The writing of fiction, the extraordinary emergence of character, teaches the writer to trust this unknown and often rejected part of the self below the surface.

We have learned that the left hemisphere of the human brain controls the right side of the body, and that side of the personality which is conscious and knowable and manipulable; whereas the right hemisphere controls the left side of the body (which is where we think of the heart as being), and that side of the personality which is intuitive and poetic. The left hand is the dreamer; the right hand is dexterous, but the left hand is sinister: We are afraid of it. We would rather not recognize how paradoxical our bodies are. The right controls the left, and the left controls the right. The camera of the eye is so constructed that we see things upside down, and then the brain has to take over and flash the vision to us right side up —which is one of the activities of the storyteller: take that which is upside down and turn it right side up; or, take that which is right side up and turn it upside down, which may be the right way to look at it after all.

The Mysterious Appearance of Canon Tallis

In *Dragons in the Waters*, Canon Tallis is kidnapped and dumped in the midst of the Venezuelan jungle, where he is attacked by a wild boar, and with enormous effort manages to kill it with a spear he has made by sharpening the end of a long stick. The man from whom this character springs has, as far as I know, never been to Venezuela, nor encountered a wild beast. Yet I realize, now that the book is finished and out of my hands, that in the spiritual jungle he has been attacked by beasts more dangerous than wild boars. Upside down may well help us to understand right side up. The ecclesiastical wilderness is fraught with as many dangers as the Venezuelan jungle, although we may have to turn to the sinister side ruled by the dextral hemisphere in order to understand this.

I wonder if it is in the dextral hemisphere that memory is stored? An alive, acute, vast memory is essential to the writer of fiction. The storyteller must remember vividly every year of life, and not be limited to the present chronological age. It is not permissible to forget what we felt and thought at 5 or 13 or 17 or 31 or 57 or . . .

A number of teen-agers have said to me, ruefully, that their parents no longer remember what it was like to be young, and they are not willing to make the effort to remember. I am learning that there is a very understandable reason for this.

A young friend of mine who is both priest and psychiatrist told me, one day when we were discussing the need for memory in storytelling, that many of his patients are afraid to delve into their memories; they are terrified of uncovering who they really are.

I think it quite likely that were I not a struggling Christian I might find it unbearable, too. But if, as a Christian, I must first and foremost accept that God loves me, warts and all, then I may be able to bear looking at these warts, some of which are revolting, suppurating and deathly. To be a Christian means to believe in the ultimate transfiguration of all matter, even the most broken and hideous. No matter what I uncover, it can, through incomprehensible grace, become the expression of God's Word and Spirit.

Without memory, terrifying and revealing though it may be, we would no longer be human, and those who forget the past become, at best, subhuman. The novelist must have at his fingertips a vast range of emotions, and some of these emotions may be savage and devastating, but anyone who hopes to be a writer may not ignore them.

Our son told us that he had learned in school about an operation which is occasionally performed on violent mental patients who have not responded to any other kind of treatment. A small incision is made in the brain (which hemisphere? the right? I wonder), and the patient's uncontrollable violence vanishes; but the patient is left with a memory span of no more than ten minutes.

I find this difficult to conceive. I cannot quite imagine what it would be like to have my past cut off ten minutes ago. Would I remember my name? Would I remember any of the books I have read? Would I know my mother, my father, husband or wife, children or friends? I only know that I would no longer be a human being. I am not even certain that I would, in any sense I can understand, be conscious. To be conscious—*conscious*—means to know *with* someone, and this implies that we cannot know alone, or without being able to remember the one with whom we know. Edward West says that a Christian is someone who knows one. A Christian is someone who can hand on the memory.

The extraordinary grace is evident in that as we tell the story, if we listen to it carefully, the memory may return. We become enabled to remember things we never knew. Although I do not understand this, I do know that it happens. It seems to me that this is what Jung is implying in his theory of the racial memory. One of the most devastating things that "modern" civilization has done is to denigrate memory. We either ignore the background of our parents and grandparents, or we idolize it with overattention to geneological charts. Or, what is worse, we discard it, by putting the guardians of the memory in nursing homes and homes for the aged. Whereas, in "primitive" societies the old people of the tribe are revered because they are the guardians of the memory. We need to recover this honoring of the memory.

I have been fascinated by Plato's theory that all learning is remembering. Education consists in drawing from the sleeping memory that which appears to have been forgotten. Hence the teacher's prime job is to awaken the memory.

This awakening of the memory is also the basis of the writing of fiction and the creation of character. My understanding of incarnation involves "anamnesis." Because I am a storyteller and have no formal training in theology, my understanding of anamnesis is that of a storyteller and not of a theologian. Anamnesis: against amnesia. But my remembering is not a vague stirring up of dormant memory so that I can look back on the past; it is indeed a re-membering; a complete reliving in the present of that which was once past. If, in a story, I must move into the understanding and awareness and dazzlement that was mine at 15, I do not just look back at it from my present lofty age; within this current moment I still *am* 15. And as I understand *anamnesis* in story, so I understand it in the Holy Mysteries. In *kairos*, "God's time," as against *chronos*, "man's time," all still *is*. There is no past tense.

Perhaps this is the right place to point out that the three Tallis novels are called juvenile novels, although this is at least to a certain extent a misnomer. The field of juvenile literature has changed radically in the past decade, and a large number of books are published as juvenile novels today which only a short time ago would have been on the adult list. Two of my juvenile novels were originally written for and published as adult novels.

However, I was aware when writing the Tallis novels, that they would be published as juvenile books, and I feel that this is a strength rather than a weakness. Children will read and accept stories which would be frightening to their parents.

Adults do not like having the status quo threatened; they really are not interested in new ideas which might shake them and shove them in new directions. Their minds are too often set in early adulthood, so that they are no longer intellectually capable of grasping fresh scientific or philosophical concepts. But children—from ten to ninety—have not closed their windows and bolted their doors. New ideas excite, rather than upset. And I remember that Jesus of Nazareth thanked God that he hid his wisdom from the old and knowledgable, and revealed it to children.

When I think of the children's books which I have loved best, I realize that they are written on a great many levels. The first level is the story; a work of fiction must hold the interest —it must be, first and foremost, a good story. Underneath that good story which keeps the reader turning the pages, is buried treasure. No one person will find all of the treasure, but each will discover special joys. I don't know enough about chess to get the full fun with Alice as she walks through the great chess board which is the world on the other side of the looking glass, but my small knowledge of mathematics enhances my pleasure. My own fumbling attempts at prayer help me to a deeper understanding of the beautiful scene in *The Wind in the Willows*, where Mole and Rat go to the island and encounter the great god Pan. George Macdonald's storytelling offers psychological insight unusual for his period. A handshake has never been an ordinary thing since Curdie was given the gift of feeling the real person as he shook hands: sometimes he would hold a snake, sometimes a cruel talon, and occasionally the trusting hand of a child.

Dante said that his great works of fantasy must be understood on four different levels: the literal level, the moral level, the allegorical level and the anagogical level. The anagogical level is the most difficult to define, but I find that it comes clear to me if I think of the allegorical level and the anagogical level as representing the two great tools of imagery, the simile and the metaphor. The "allegorical" level corresponds to simile; it shows us what something is *like*. Whereas the "anagogical" level corresponds to metaphor; it shows us what something *is*. Only the greatest writers serve the anagogical level as it should be served. I was horrified to hear a lecturer in poetry say that there really isn't much difference between a simile and a metaphor. But to say that Jesus is like God is not at all the same thing as to say that Jesus *is* God.

The anagogical level is approached only when the mind is deep in the heart, only when intellect and intuition are no longer in conflict. I do not believe that any writer can consciously explore the anagogical level; it is sheer grace.

But grace is a terrifying idea to secular man; we do not like thinking that we are not in control. A child has no problem in accepting this. A baby has no say about who his parents ought to be, or in what country he will be born, or what language he is to speak. He is not in charge of what he is fed or what he wears. Perhaps the child does not realize that his Olympian parents have only an iota more of control, but at least children realize their dependence and understand their freedom. As Dean Inge said, "God promised to make man free; he never promised to make him independent." A child understands that this freedom is sheer grace, and so walks intuitively in an anagogical world.

There is nothing more likely to raise the blood pressure of a lover of children's books than the average adult's unspoken premise that one does not write for children if one is good enough to write for adults. Fear of the multileveled world is masked in intolerant condescension. This denigration of the writer of children's books is pervasive. Last June I taught the Juveniles Workshop at a Writer's Conference—one of the best conferences I know about, and where I have taught several times before. Something came more sharply to my attention this time than other summers, and this was the peculiar quality of the juvenile manuscripts. I had twenty-eight manuscripts to read before the week of the conference, and during that week there were twenty-eight individual sessions with the writers, as well as the daily hour-long lectures.

In the first lecture, I stressed, as I always do, that the techniques for writing junior novels are exactly the same as those for writing adult novels, and that many authors write for more than one market. I had had two successful adult novels published before I dared try my hand at a junior novel, and I still move back and forth between the two fields. One has to be feeling strong and full of courage to write fantasy, such as *A Wrinkle In Time* or *A Wind in the Door*.

Something in many of the manuscripts which came to me last summer bothered me, and I couldn't put my finger on what it was. Many were adequately written, several more than adequately, but there was still something wrong with the majority of them, and I didn't know what.

I found out on the last day of the conference when all the lectures are open, and the lecturers for the various workshops have a chance to listen to one another. Many of the students take several workshops; a number of my students were in each of the workshops I attended that day. The leaders read some of the work aloud, and suddenly, as I listened to the stories, the poems, the sections of novels written by the men and women who had been in my juveniles workshop and whose manuscripts I had read so carefully, I realized what had been bothering me: in writing for children most of these people had been writing down, not so much writing down to children as writing down to themselves. They were writing below their own capacity, in style, characterization, conception. I was so outraged after hearing a short story by a young man who had turned in a dull piece of work for the juveniles workshop that I went up to him after class and figuratively shook him as I said, "The way you wrote that short story is the way you write for children, not the way you wrote that thing you turned in to me. Why do you think that when you write for children you should write less well than you are able to write?"

A few weeks after the writer's conference last summer, I went to teach a seminar on techniques of fiction at a midwestern university. Halfway through the second day, one of the students said, "I hope you're going to teach us something about writing for children. That's what I'm really taking this class for."

"What have I been teaching you?"

"Well—writing."

"Don't you write when you write for children?"

"Well, I guess so, yes—but isn't it a lot different?"

No, I told her. No, it is not. Beatrix Potter and Fyodor Dostoevsky would have understood each other.

"Well, what about vocabulary? Shouldn't vocabulary be easier for children? I mean long words and sentences and stuff."

Mark Twain said that he never used the word metropolis when he could use the word city. Whether one is writing for adults or children the simplest word is almost always the best word. When a complicated word is essential for what the writer needs to convey, then in the context it is the simplest and only word.

"Tesseract" (which is a real word) is not found on any limited vocabulary lists, but I couldn't have written *A Wrinkle in Time* without it. *Kything,* which is essential for *A Wind in the Door,* is a word I have come across only in an ancient Scottish dictionary. After I wrote *A Wind* I had a letter from a young man at Harvard saying, "I think I like it better than *Wrinkle,* but I feel I ought to warn you that this is going to be a very difficult book for many adults."

Why?

Not, I suppose, because I use a few scientific concepts, like mitochondrion. *Wrinkle* and *A Wind* are fantasy, and fantasy must be solidly grounded in reality before it can take off. More likely it is because these books explore scientific ideas which lead in the direction of new philosophical and theological ideas, and children are far more willing to expose themselves to new ideas than many of their parents are. So when a book full of new ideas comes to me and asks me to write it, I'm likely to write it for children—and all this means as far as the technique of fiction is concerned is that my protagonist is usually somewhere between twelve and twenty.

No, not quite all. There is one other thing. In a book for children I am as careful about vocabulary, syntax, style, characterization, structure, as I am in an adult novel, but in the book for children there is one thing that I may not do: I may not despair. I may show a great deal that is wrong in this world. My protagonist may have to hurt a great deal in order to grow and deepen; but there is below all that happens a Yes to the fact of existence. With Julian of Norwich I try to affirm that all shall be well and all manner of things shall be well.

I'm not sure that I think despair is permissible in an adult novel either, though many are published which wallow in despair. However these strike me as being rough first drafts rather than works of art. No one could have been more ruthless in exploring the depravity of the human heart than Dostoevsky, who wrote many drafts of each of his books, and who should be read by all who hope to write for children. Despite the brutal realism of his novels, ultimately Dostoevsky says Yes! to Creation. We human beings may be, and often are, all wrong; but there is something which is all right, and this all rightness makes everything bearable—and possible.

When the irregularities in the orbit of Uranus were discovered, it seemed to indicate that something was all wrong in the heavens. There appeared to be no reason for such unstructured behavior on the part of a planet in a reliable solar system. Many scientists threw up their hands in horror and cried that the heavens were in a mess. However, the great scientist, Leverrier, with faith in the basic all rightness of the universe, computed the size, position and orbit of a planet which, if the strange irregularity of Uranus were to make sense, must be in the sky. Because Leverrier had a fundamental faith that the universe is not irrational, he risked predicting that Neptune had to be there. And so it was, a hitherto undiscovered planet, causing the seemingly meaningless irregularities in Uranus.

It is all right, Leverrier was assuring himself and the rest of the world. There is meaning. It is all right.

It is this same faith in the ultimate all rightness of things which sends me to the typewriter, no matter how wrong everything around me may be. In a world which sometimes seems to be without hope, I still affirm hope.

Thus the writer of the true children's book is somewhat like Leverrier: he looks at the world and sees man's intolerable cruelty to man; the wicked flourish and the innocent suffer; children pay dearly for the stupidity and viciousness of adults. But the children's writer does not throw up his hands in horror at the chaos. Instead, he creates story and pattern and perspective and so, like Leverrier looking for the creative and positive cause of the irregular behavior of Uranus, he discovers not a sentimental and therefore untrue happy ending, but something as solid as a planet.

Leverrier had to know the techniques of science and mathematics in order to acquire the ability to discover Neptune. The writer of children's fiction, no less than the adult novelist, must know the techniques of the craft and must, like the scientist, have a point of view.

Leverrier thought in particulars, not in generalities. It is strange to me, therefore, that philosophers and theologians so often talk in generalities. Yet it is only the scandal of the particular which pushes back the mists of generalities. Particularity is frightening, there's no denying that. But if it shows me depths of depravity I hardly knew existed, it also shows me courage and nobility and endurance. And it pulls me, willy-nilly, into the excitement of participating in a universe which is still being created (God, as Edward West points out, says "I will be what I will be"), and in which each one of us, like every grain of sand, like every whirling galaxy, has his own role.

There we go again—role. Too often, because we are the protagonist of our own little lives, we make the mistake of thinking that we are the protagonist of the play, or even that we write the script. But when we turn mind and memory to the true Author of our being, we move toward our true vocation of serving, and occasionally, collaborating.

My husband plays a role. I tell a story. But rather than acting or writing a lie, we become discoverers. I may not discover the means to light the fire or the words of the prayer, and I may be too lost to find the forest, much less the place within it.

But when a story comes to me, peopled with characters, even those I do not choose to write about, I will try to tell it.

3

Rest and Restlessness in
Christian Spirituality

John Macquarrie

THE ANCIENT CITY of Basel possesses a beautiful minster, standing high above the Rhine on a site where Christian worship has been offered continuously since about the year 800. Basel's reformer, Oecolampadius, was a humanist, and so the minster's statues, monuments and carvings were largely spared at the time when iconoclasts were busy elsewhere. But one curious modification did occur. On the west front of the minster, on the north side of the great door, can be seen St. George on horseback, thrusting his spear into the dragon. On the south side of the door is another horseman, but he is in isolation, and one feels that something is missing. In fact, this other horseman is St. Martin, and originally the group was balanced by the figure of the beggar to whom St. Martin gave his cloak. But at the time of the Reformation, the beggar was removed. The reasoning was that this public display of St. Martin performing a meritorious act might lead the people to the mistaken belief that they could gain salvation through good works. So for the past four hundred years, St. Martin has been riding on by himself, doing nothing at all. And this *dolce far niente* proclaims for all who can understand such matters the glorious truth of *sola gratia*—that we are saved by grace alone, and not through works.

Nowadays when we hear this little story we find it rather amusing. Nevertheless, it draws our attention to two important facts about our Christian religion. The first is that in matters both of faith and practice we find ourselves in a tension of opposites, so that we have to live and believe dialectically, not letting go either side but recognizing that both have just claims upon us. For instance, in matters of faith, we have to acknowledge that God is transcendent and yet he is immanent, that he is one and yet he is three, that our Lord Jesus Christ is divine and yet he is human, that he is the eternal Word and yet that he was born and lived on this earth at a particular time in history; and so we could go on. Likewise, in matters of practice, we have to acknowledge the apparently conflicting claims of contemplation and action, of worship and service to others, of private morality and commitment to social or political ideals—and again we could go on listing the contrasts. The second fact is that when placed in this dialectical situation, neither the Church as a whole nor individual Christians have been notably successful in facing up to the total demand in all its complexity. Usually the tension has been relaxed and some onesided simplistic solution has been adopted, as happened in the case of those Basel reformers who thought that the sovereignty of the divine grace could be safeguarded only by discouraging good works.

Of course, in any given situation, one side or other of the dialectic may need to be emphasized to make up for earlier neglect. Some exaggeration seems inevitable, and if one were ever to reach a state of equilibrium, this might well turn out to be a kind of death, in which the dynamic had gone out of Christianity and further advance had become impossible. But it is quite another matter to so exaggerate one side of the dialectic that one becomes almost totally insensitive to the other. But this is what often happens in the history of the Church—the so-called swing of the pendulum. A truly catholic theology and spirituality try to maintain the wholeness of the Christian heritage, while freely acknowledging that different items in that heritage may need to be stressed at different times.

It is a curious irony that the Protestant thrust, which went to such exaggerated lengths at the time of the Reformation in stressing the *sola fide* principle and in correspondingly deemphasizing good works, has in our own day gone to the opposite extreme, for now we hear of nothing but activism and involvement in public affairs. The most shattering indictment of this new onesidedness has come from a distinguished theologian in the Reformed tradition, Professor Thomas F. Torrance of Edinburgh. He sees "the vast slide of Church leaders in recent times into something like an obsession with socio-moral concerns" and their desire for "consciously meritorious involvement in socio-political issues" as concomitant with a decay of the inward substance of faith and so with a need for self-justification. Professor Torrance goes on: "I am more and more staggered at two things: first, the astonishing *volte-face* that has been taking place in the Churches of the Reformation, in that they reveal a serious lapse from the centrality of the gospel of Christ, together with a failure to understand that it is justification by grace alone which creates the ethical disturbance that turns the world upside down; and, secondly, the growing contradiction that the Western Churches exhibit to Jesus' total rejection of every value system based on power, and his proclamation of the new order, which cannot be brought about by any form of force, together with a failure to remember that Jesus was crucified by contemporaries who bitterly resented his refusal to have anything whatsoever to do with their political theology."[1] Of course, the prevailing drive toward justification by works is not confined to the Protestant Churches but has many sympathizers among Roman Catholics.

The tendencies described are to be seen in Churches all over the world, but they seem to have assumed a particularly acute form in the American Churches. Pragmatism has for long been a powerful force in the United States, and ideas are valued to the extent that they can be set to work. On the other hand, anything savoring of quietism has been suspect.

But must we always be blown about by extremes of doctrine and practice? Can we not learn to become at once more dialectical and more catholic? Is it so very difficult to entertain more than one idea at a time? Has Anglicanism, traditionally the *via media*, something to teach the other branches of the Christian Church on these matters? And if we have to emphasize one element of truth more than another, is it not more important to acknowledge our receptiveness in the presence of God than our own doing?

These questions bring me to the particular contrast which forms the theme of this essay—rest and restlessness in the Christian life. They lead me also at this point to acknowledge my debt to Canon Edward West, in whose honor this volume of essays has been produced. At the time when I was preparing for ordination to the priesthood, Canon West was my guide and counselor on all questions relating to prayer, liturgy and spirituality. He even entrusted me with the loan of his own personally annotated prayer book. There can be very few people in the Anglican Communion who approach Canon West in his profound knowledge and understanding of these matters. So often, too, those who are deemed "knowledgable" in liturgy and spirituality are found to be conversant with the history of the subject, possibly even in great detail, but to have little understanding for the theological issues and for what one might call more broadly the philosophy of worship. Canon West knows the history but equally he understands the principles. For this reason, he was able to explain to me in a way that made a great deal of sense the ideas underlying the movement for liturgical renewal. Yet just because he understood and sympathized with the true motives of the liturgical reformers, he was also aware of the distortions and exaggerations that have come about where new practices have been adopted without a genuine understanding of their purpose. I remember that on one occasion when he had been talking about liturgical reform, he paused for a moment and said: "But it can all become very Pelagian." That remark surely goes to the very heart of the matter.

Rest and restlessness, contemplation and action, prayer and service, grace and works, serenity and concern—all of these have their place in Christian life and spirituality, yet they are always in tension, and it is never easy to order the priorities. To be sure, we have to think in terms that go beyond individual experience, and remembering that the Church is a corporate entity in which different members do different things, we can acknowledge that some by temperament and calling fulfill their discipleship chiefly in the contemplative life, others in the life of action. Yet when this has been said, it does not take away the problem for the individual. Everyone's Christian discipleship needs some balance if it is not to become a distorted caricature. Each one of us has to learn to strike somehow the balance between the apparently equally valid claims of contemplation and action.

For what religion worthy of the name does not hold out to its devotees the promise of rest, peace and serenity? Herein lies much of the appeal of religion. We are finite creatures, largely at the mercy of circumstances over which we have little control. We are harassed by the continual threats that attend our transient mode of existence. Amid all these threats, we long to be able to cling to a rock that is higher than ourselves, to experience an inward tranquility and assurance that will give the lie to all the appearances of evil in the world. Is it just weakness that stirs such a desire in us? Or is it part of the meaning of finitude that we must look beyond ourselves and seek a ground on which we can rest? Christianity has never been ashamed of responding to this cry of the human heart. Our Lord himself told his disciples that his parting gift to them was peace. For centuries, Christian devotion has talked of resting in Jesus, of casting care upon him and so on. All this constitutes, at the very least, an ineluctable part of Christian spiritual history. If this is weakness and neurosis, so be it—but there is no way that it can be dissociated from the Christian tradition. And is it not the case that the Christians who impress us most deeply are precisely those who have developed a certain serenity and inner quiet, so that they can give us confidence when we turn to them? To whom do we go for counsel when we are at our wit's end and the world is falling to pieces around us? We go, as likely as not, to someone who has been formed in what we call the religious life. His mind we find to be like a sacred space where wisdom and sanity still prevail and the madness of the world has not penetrated. And we turn to such Christians because we believe that through their spiritual discipline they have become in some measure like God. Every man and woman is made in the image of God, and Christian discipleship consists in strengthening and developing that image through conforming us to Christ, who is the express image of God in a human existence. We cannot speak of God unless there is a real sense in which God endures unchanging through the changes and chances that beset our eathly existence. Part of the meaning of the very word "God" is that it denotes one whose being is like an infinite calm transcending the storms of time and history. And the end of the Christian life has also been visualized in terms of rest. *"Requiem aeternam dona eis. . . . "* Our prayer is that the departed, after all the pains and struggles of their life on earth, may attain to the vision of God and to participation in his life, and so to the peace that passes understanding. And we believe that even now, in the midst of the struggle, in moments of intense awareness of God, we glimpse the vision and know the peace and enjoy, as it were, a corner of heaven on earth.

All I have said about rest and peace in that long paragraph is true. And yet, as soon as it has been said, we recognize that almost every point needs to be qualified by saying something else which seems to contradict it, but seems, nevertheless, to be equally true. Granted that Christianity, like every religion, offers peace, we have still to ask, "What kind of peace?" There is a hymn familiar to American church people that turns it all around, and suggests that before the coming of Christ among them, the first Galilean disciples were simple, happy contented folk. "The peace of God, it is no peace, but strife closed in the sod."[2] And now we have to remember that although Christ promised the gift of peace to his followers, he told them also that for his sake they would have to undergo strife and tribulation. So when we talk of rest or peace or serenity as belonging to the essence of Christianity, we can never mean a rest that is just content with things as they are or a peace that means dropping out from the real world and its problems. And when we think more deeply of God himself, although we could not go back on the belief that it is of the very nature of God to transcend the storms that beset finite existence, we must also say that it is of the very nature of the God we have known in Jesus Christ to be alongside his creatures in their suffering. His impassibility could never be understood in any way that would make him an "apathetic" God, in the modern sense of that adjective. This God of infinite calm and rest is at the same time the God who grieves for his children and yearns for them. And finally, though the end of the Christian life is rest in God, this cannot be a rest in which nothing further will ever happen—that would be a kind of death. Rather, as a great master of the spiritual life, St. Gregory of Nyssa, taught, the very perfection of the Christian life is a never-ending advance into the inexhaustible riches of God.

There are the two sides of the truth of rest and restlessness. I doubt if we can synthesize them into a greater, comprehensive truth. Perhaps that kind of understanding is reserved to God alone, or to ourselves only when we have come much nearer to God than we ever are *in via*. For the present, we can only hope to be sensitive to both sides of the truth, and to respond to all its dimensions. Again, if we remember individual differences, we shall not all respond in the same way. We must avoid the temptation to decry the person who responds differently, or to think that our way is the better way, still less the only way. The activist is sadly in error when he despises the man or woman who spends a large part of his time at prayer or in church, and the most obvious proof of this is the fact noted above, that people in trouble turn for help to those whose inner serenity makes it plain that their lives are rooted in a reality deeper than the flux of everyday events. But the contemplative spirit may be equally in error if he censors the activist for being rarely in church or engaged in formal prayer, though he may be very fully engaged in the Lord's business. However, it is perhaps again significant that contemplatives are much less frequently censorious than are activists, for it is part of their wisdom to have a broad compassionate grasp of the endless varieties of human nature.

Still, if the trend at present is in the direction of activism and restlessness, there is a special duty to consider again the claims of contemplation and the value of rest. We now turn to such a consideration, and we shall carry it out in three stages, beginning from a broad perspective and then narrowing down to some of the matters that lie at the center.

We begin then with the broad perspective, and ask in a general way about the place of prayer and worship in the life of the ordinary Christian. What time ought he to give to them? What priority ought he to accord to them? How are the claims for time of prayer and worship to be reconciled with the claims of action? Such questions have been raised in a somewhat aggressive way in recent years, and although we do not hear as much as we did about a so-called secular Christianity, many people do seem to believe that Christianity consists primarily in good works, and that the rest is a kind of spiritual luxury, and one that we ought to do without in days when there is so much to be done in service to mankind.

In the first place, I think we must get away from any idea that our time and our loyalty are somehow to be "divided" between competing claims. Just to recall for a moment the New Testament witness, we see our Lord working to the point of physical exhaustion among the people, and we see him retiring into desert places to recollect himself in quiet, but there is no question of any conflict between these two aspects of his ministry. They constitute an undivided whole. So too it ought to be in the lives of his followers. The cultivation of the life of the spirit is not a turning away from the demands and challenges of the active life. The two are continuous. I like to use the word "concentration" to point to what prayer and worship bring about. These are times when we bring to explicit awareness that relation to Jesus Christ that is present all the time. In this sense, we could describe these as times of consciousness raising, to use a popular expression. They do not introduce something different, but they concentrate in its intensity that orientation to Jesus Christ present in a diffuse way throughout the whole of the disciple's living and acting. Those theologians who urge us to see God in the neighbor and in the everyday situations of life are perfectly correct in what they affirm—indeed, they are simply commending what has been traditionally called "habitual recollection," which means living all the time in the presence of God. But some of them feel that they have also got to decry the special times of prayer and the special religious occasions, and they are mistaken in what they deny, for I do not think that one can recognize God in the ordinary situations where he is veiled unless one has first learned to know him in those situations where we stand before him in the revealing moment of word or sacrament or prayer. Habitual recollection comes only after one has submitted to the disciplines of the spiritual life.

In the second place, those who would devalue prayer and worship seem to imagine that the Christian life is far easier than it actually is. Perhaps they themselves are *naturaliter Christiani*, and find it no trouble to give themselves in love to the neighbor or to be men and women for others. But I suspect that with most people it is very different. There is less emphasis in Christian theology today on sin than there was in the generation of Reinhold Niebuhr and Karl Barth, but sin has not gone away. Nations, individuals, social classes, racial and ethnic blocs, economic groups—all of these today display just as much hardness and self-interest as ever they did. Christianity does not come easily to any of them. The idea that one can just go out and love one's neighbor is incredibly naïve, and it has not even yet begun to consider what love is—and surely there is no more abused word in the language than this word "love." The meaning of love and still more the doing of it have to be learned or, better, received, before we can become agents of love. As Tom Torrance pointed out in the passage quoted earlier, there has to take place the radical disturbance or displacement of grace if the Christian ethic of love is to be released into the world. Let me say again, however, that there must be no division, not even a division into cause and effect. The relation of grace and ethic, of prayer and act, is a reciprocal one. It is knowledge of God in Christ and daily communing with him that sensitizes one for the ordinary situations of life; but on the other hand, these ordinary situations lead into a deeper existential knowledge of God in Christ. To put it in another way, if we have spent time reading the Bible, we shall be better able to respond with compassion and understanding to the current human situations as we find it set forth in today's *New York Times;* but it will be that concrete human situation that will bring alive for us the Bible's teaching.

Advocates of secular Christianity often appeal to the example of Dietrich Bonhoeffer on the basis of some rather obscure passages in his letters, but I think that in fact he illustrates much more convincingly that reciprocity of prayer and action, of rest and restlessness, which I am commending here. Dr. Michael Ramsey has given careful consideration to those passages in Bonhoeffer's letters which support the idea of a "religionless" Christianity, and in response to the question whether these passages can really be held to represent Bonhoeffer's mind on the matter, Dr. Ramsey says this: "My own answer is found largely in many other passages in Bonhoeffer's *Letters and Papers from Prison,* and reading the letters as a whole, I find two things vividly impressed me. First, that God is found in the tragedy of the world, far outside the religious camp. Second, that for all Bonhoeffer says about religion, religion is growing powerfully in his own soul. Again and again in his letters, he is expressing his dependence upon God through the medium of his own memory of hymns and psalms and music, the rhythms of the Christian year, the stuff of the worshiping tradition." Dr. Ramsey quotes extensively from the letters to support his point, and draws attention to "the submissiveness which is the mark of the religious man." But he pushes the matter further: "Is this religious element so strongly present in Bonhoeffer's letters a kind of hangover from that immaturity from which, he says, the Christian must move onwards? No, the religion disclosed in the letters seems to me far from retrogressive. Rather does it seem to mount from strength to strength."[3] One might add to Dr. Ramsey's testimony that of the camp doctor who was present at Bonhoeffer's execution: "Through the half-open door in one room of the huts I saw Pastor Bonhoeffer, before taking off his prison garb, kneeling on the floor praying fervently to his God. I was most deeply moved by the way this lovable man prayed, so devout and so certain that God heard his prayer. . . . In the almost fifty years that I worked as a doctor, I have hardly ever seen a man die so entirely submissive to the will of God."[4]

Bonhoeffer's prayer, we may say, concentrated his life of discipleship, but his life gave expression to his prayer. Neither is conceivable without the other, and it is this relationship of inward submission to and rest in God with outward action in God's service that each Christian must work out in his own life in the way that will best fulfill his own discipleship.

Now we must narrow the range of our consideration. If we have established that in the Christian life there is a place for simply resting in God, for resorting to him in prayer and adoration (though this will not be isolated from the remainder of our concerns), we have still to ask about the structure of this specifically spiritual discipline itself. Traditionally, it included both participation in the public liturgy and such private acts of prayer and devotion as each person might find suited to his or her needs. But today there is strong pressure against what might be called the private sector of spirituality. And again it is the activist spirit that is exerting this pressure. The attitude seems to be: "If it has to be acknowledged that some prayer and worship are needed in the Christian life, then let us indeed make eucharist together as a corporate act, but then let us immediately return to the world and its service." Thus, whereas people used to remain kneeling in prayer for a little while after, they are now urged to leave with instant abruptness. "Go, the mass is over!" is interpreted with a literalness that hardly encourages us to see a continuity between the eucharist and life outside the sanctuary. Again, whereas the eucharist used to be the center around which there was a whole structure of offices and devotions, the tendency now is to discourage any acts of prayer and worship apart from the eucharist itself.

Of course, one cannot deny the element of truth in the current tendencies. The eucharist is the center and model for all Christian spirituality, and its restoration to the central place is one of the great achievements of recent times. In the Roman Catholic Church, the eucharist until recently was frequently smothered in the plethora of private devotions that had grown up around it. In the Anglican communion and most of the Protestant Churches, the eucharist was often displaced by a service of the word alone. Certainly, no one can complain that eucharistic worship has been gaining ground on all sides—rather one must warmly welcome this. But again, it is not what is affirmed that causes concern, but what is denied. Can the eucharist be exalted only by a devaluing of the office, devotions to the Blessed Sacrament reserved, the rosary and all the other forms of prayer that have been found helpful in the life of the Christian—precisely the forms, be it noted, which encourage the contemplative and meditative aspects of spirituality?

Thomas Merton, who in a remarkable way combined the contemplative and the active modes of life, stated bluntly: "The true fruition of the eucharist is not normally possible unless our eucharistic communion is somehow prolonged in silent and solitary adoration."[5] This is the other side of the truth, which must also be maintained in spite of all the pressures against it at the present time. We shall not "get it right," so to speak, if rest is completely swallowed up in restlessness. Dr. Hans Urs von Balthasar has put it very well: "One sees clearly where things had got on to the wrong track: the event became static, the process became a state, that which offered itself incomprehensibly became that which was offered in graspable form, that which transcended sight became that which was seen, the presence of the divine was turned into an earthly presence. All that sounds plausible. But perhaps, if we think it through more deeply, we shall not be able to bring it down to such simple formulae."[6] We hear in these words the true dialectic of Christian truth and Christian life, and we need to hear these words if we are to be delivered from the impoverishment that comes from onesidedness and oversimplification. Let us by all means ensure the centrality of the eucharist, but let us not fail to provide such other occasions of prayer and devotion as will help to extend the meaning of the eucharist into every area of life, through our profound meditation on its mysteries.

If then we have established that there is a place for appropriate acts of devotion alongside the eucharist, let us come to the final focusing of our perspective, namely, on the eucharist itself. There are many dimensions to this great Christian sacrament, and at different times in history or in different traditions of Christendom, different dimensions of the sacrament have been stressed. In our own time, the stress has come to be on what we call the "horizontal" dimension, that is to say, the sacrament seen as a common meal in which is both expressed and realized the solidarity of believers in the body of Christ. This is a true and essential part of the meaning of the eucharist, and no doubt it needed to be reasserted, for in all Christian traditions the nature of the eucharist as a truly corporate action had become obscured. But once again it is important to affirm without denying, to lay hold on the new (or newly rediscovered) enrichment without becoming insensitive to what we have known hitherto. For without its "vertical" dimension, the relation to the transcendent God, the eucharist is emptied of its power and significance.

Once more, however, it is important to see that there cannot be a rivalry here. We cannot honor God unless we are in love and charity with our neighbors; but we cannot love our neighbors as we ought unless we are lifted out of ourselves and set in orbit around God. If this essential vertical dimension is to come through clearly in our eucharistic celebrations, then we have to think again about what is happening in liturgical reform. The movement has been all in one direction. The use of informal language, the westward position of the celebrant, the elimination of the moments of penitence and humility, the prominence given to the kiss of peace and to communion as over against consecration and oblation—all these taken together have produced a massive shift in the meaning of the sacrament. There is no one of these points that cannot be defended, and perhaps no one of them has not been needed to correct earlier exaggerations. But there is no doubt that the total effect has been to let the eucharist appear chiefly as something that is going on among ourselves and that we are doing for ourselves, with God kept discreetly in the background. In this sense, Edward West's comment about Pelagianism was well taken. It is time that we gave thought to changing direction in our liturgical thinking, and to making clear that above all it is God in Christ who founds and initiates the sacramental action. And this can only be done if we find room in our rites for rest as well as action, for moments of quiet, passivity, receptiveness, humility, adoration before the mystery of the God who reaches out to us before we ever dream of turning to him and before we ever learn rightly to love each other.

Rest and restlessness both have their place in the Christian life. But of late we have had too much of the restlessness, and surely the time has come for us to learn again the value of being quietly open to God.

NOTES

1. T. F. Torrance, *Theology in Reconciliation*, 1975, pp. 277–78.
2. *The Hymnal 1940*, No. 437.
3. A. M. Ramsey, *Sacred and Secular*, 1965, pp. 52–3.
4. E. Bethge, *Dietrich Bonhoeffer*, 1970, pp. 830–31.
5. Thomas Merton, *The Silent Life*, 1957, p. 150.
6. H. U. von Balthasar, *Elucidations*, 1975, p. 119.

4

Christmas, Epiphany, and the Johannine Prologue

Reginald H. Fuller

CANON EDWARD WEST'S friends and colleagues will remember his disdain for the festival of Christmas. After a striking series of Advent sermons in the Cathedral of St. John the Divine, he would lapse into a sort of intellectual hibernation and spiritual melancholy to emerge again only at Epiphany. Edward West is profoundly influenced by Eastern Orthodoxy, for which Epiphany takes theological and liturgical precedence over Christmas. And it is the celebration of Christ's baptism, not the visit of the Magi, that engages the primary attention of the Orthodox. The thesis of this paper, written in honor of Edward West, will be that this insight is true to the New Testament as well.

We shall seek to accomplish our purpose by a consideration of the Johannine Prologue and its Christology, concluding with a brief comparison of that Christology with the Christology of the infancy narratives in Matthew and Luke. In a recent essay to be published elsewhere,[1] I have tried to show that Johannine Christology operates at two levels, in contrast to the later doctrine of the two natures of Christ. The Christology of the Fourth Gospel is, on one level, an historical one. Jesus in his history from baptism to glorification was the Epiphany of the divine wisdom, a mythological concept developed in pre-Christian Judaism. This two-level presentation of the person of Christ is first hinted at in John 3:13 and then developed in the "Bread discourse" of John 6. This gives two distinct levels to Jesus' history: he is at once an historical figure, sent by God to perform a unique role in salvation history, and at the same time, that role is to incarnate the mythological figure of the divine wisdom which descended from heaven.

The notion that it is the baptism rather than the birth of Jesus which marks the point of wisdom's entry into the world not only seems shockingly suggestive of adoptionism, but contrary to the Johannine Prologue, with its climactic affirmation, "the Word became flesh" (John 1:14). Surely, the *egeneto* must refer to the moment of Jesus' nativity or his conception. But does it really? We get the impression that it does largely because of its use as the liturgical gospel of the third Mass of Christmas Day. But there is no annunciation story in the Fourth Gospel, and no nativity or infancy narrative either. The Prologue is immediately followed by the witness of the Baptist to the inner meaning of Jesus' baptism[2]. This means that the Prologue is a commentary not on the birth of Jesus, but in the first instance, on the baptism and more remotely on the ministry of Jesus in its entirety. It cannot be other than a commentary on what follows, not on what is absent from the book!

This interpretation of the Prologue is supported by a form-critical and traditio-critical study of the Prologue itself. It has for some time been recognized that the Prologue is a hymn in verse form or at least in rhythmic prose. This hymn has been expanded with prose insertions at a later stage in its history. It is largely through the influence of R. Bultmann's commentary on the Gospel of John that the hymnic origin of the

Prologue has established itself. Bultmann, however, was of the opinion that the hymn originated in "baptist" circles where their founder was revered in terms of the pre-Christian gnostic redeemer myth. The Evangelist, supposedly a convert from these circles, brought along the hymn and adapted it to his new faith in Jesus. Together with other additions, the Evangelist inserted verses 6–8 and 15 as a polemical rejection of his previous identification of the Logos with the Baptist.

Few today would hold Bultmann's views on the Prologue in their entirety. The theory of a pre-Christian gnostic redeemer myth has been demolished by the researches of C. Colpe and others.[4] On sheer chronological grounds, it is highly improbable, for all of Bultmann's supporting evidence is later than the New Testament. As he once remarked to the present writer, the earliest evidence for the gnostic redeemer myth is the Fourth Gospel! All examples of the gnostic redeemer myth are later than the New Testament and reflect the influence of Christinaity. Hence there can be no question that the Baptist was ever regarded in New Testament times as the incarnation of the preexistent Logos. Furthermore, it is equally questionable whether the Mandaean literature can be used as evidence for the identification of the Baptist with the gnostic redeemer, even at a later date.

An alternative view seems to be increasingly establishing itself. According to this, the Johannine Prologue grew out of the Jewish wisdom tradition, probably in its Hellenistic form.[5] But it is, at least as taken over by the Fourth Evangelist, already a *Christianized* Wisdom-Logos hymn. This is how the hymn is reconstructed by R. Schnackenburg:

I

(vs. 1)   In the beginning was the Logos,
             and the Logos was with God,
             and the Logos was God.

(vs. 3)   All things were made by him,
             and without him was made
             nothing that was made.

II

(vs. 4)　In him was life,
　　　　and the life was the light of men.
(vs. 9)　He was the true light
　　　　that enlightens every man.

III

(vs. 10)　He was in the world,
　　　　and the world knew him not.
(vs. 11)　He came to his own,
　　　　and his own received him not.

IV

(vs. 14)　And the Logos became flesh,
　　　　and tabernacled among us,
　　　　full of grace and truth.
(vs. 16)　For (and) of his fullness
　　　　we all received,
　　　　grace upon grace.[6]

This pre-Johannine Christian hymn covers the following points:

(1) The divine nature of the preexistent Logos and his priority over all creation (vs. 1).

(2) The Logos as the agent of creation (vs. 3).

(3) The Logos' special relationship to humanity, the source of life and revelation (vss. 4, 9).

(4) The conflict between the Logos as revelation and humanity in its rejection of the revelation (vss. 10–11).

(5) The incarnation of the Logos and the plenary revelation it brought (vss. 14, 16). In traditional terms, sections (1)–(4) speak of the *Logos asarkos,* that is, "the preincarnate" Logos, and only (5) of the Logos *ensarkos.* Since this hymn originally stood on its own, completely detached from any specific context in the earthly life of Jesus, its concluding affirmation "the Logos became flesh" will have looked back upon that earthly life in its entirety, not to any specific moment in it. The *sarx* will have covered "the whole observable history of Jesus"

(Hoskyns), and the aorist *egeneto*, "was made," will have been a complexive aorist.[7]

The Evangelist then took up this hymn and used it as a prelude to his gospel as a whole, and more specifically to his account of the Baptist's witness, which follows in verses 19–36, and in a way continues through verse 51. He also interpolated a number of prose additions and other phrases which disturb the original poetic structure of the hymn. These include verses 12–13 and 17–18, which exhibit Johannine characteristica[8]. These additions are not immediately relevant to our concern, however. We will concentrate rather on the two prose insertions which refer to John the Baptist:

> There was a man sent from God, whose name was John. He came for testimony, to bear witness to the light, that all might believe through him. He was not the light, but came to bear witness to the light . . . John bore witness to him, and cried, "This was he of whom I said, 'He who comes after me ranks before me, for he was before me.' " (John 1:6–8, 15)

Three questions need to be answered: (1) What is the source of these passages? Are they the Evangelist's own composition, or did he take them from an earlier source? (2) What was the Evangelist's intention in inserting these passages into the hymn? (3) What changes do these interpolations make to the meaning of the hymn?

(1) Charles Masson[9] made the interesting suggestion that in the first draft of his gospel the Evangelist began straightaway with the witness of the Baptist, and that his account of that witness began with verses 6–8 and 15, as they now stand, followed immediately by verse 19.[10] This then is how the gospel, in its first draft, would have begun:

> There was a man sent from God whose name was John. He came for a testimony, to bear witness to the light, that all might believe through him. He was not that light, but came to bear witness to that light. John bore witness to him and cried, "He who comes after me ranks before me, for he was before me." And this is the

testimony of John, when the Jews sent priests and Levites from Jerusalem to ask him, "Who are you?" He confessed, he did not deny, but confessed, "I am not the Christ."[11]

It is clear that this original beginning of the gospel is thoroughly Johannine. It exhibits such characteristica as "witness,"[12] "light" as a Christological term[13] and "believe."[14] It asserts the preexistence of the light that was incarnate in Jesus.[15] More particularly, it launches an apologetic against the continuing "Baptists" who evidently regarded their founder as a messianic figure, though not, as Bultmann suggested, as the incarnation of the preexistent gnostic revealer.[16] This apologetic is sustained through the early chapters of the gospel.[17] Impregnated though they are with Johannine characteristica, verses 6–8 and 15 also enshrine material of a non-Johannine character. First, the phrase "there was a man sent from God whose name is John" is contrary to the Fourth Evangelist's normal practice of restricting the terminology of sending to Christ—an inconsistency which led E. Haenchen mistakenly to ascribe verses 6–8 to a post-Johannine redactor, though he was right to spot the inconsistency.[18] The more obvious explanation is that "a man sent from God" was the opening phrase of the Evangelist's source. It has an Old Testament-Semitic ring, reminiscent of the similar opening to the account of the Baptist's ministry in Luke 3:1.[19] The second interpolation, verse 15, also enshrines traditional material in the phrase "he who comes after me." Verses 6–8 and 15 are in their present form so overlaid with Johannine theology that it is impossible to disentangle and reconstruct their original pre-Johannine form.

(2) In their original position the purpose of these verses about the Baptist was, as we have seen, apologetic. Transposed, and inserted into the hymn, they are still apologetic,[20] but the fact that the hymn goes beyond the theology of the Baptist's verses indicates that their interpolation had more than the purely apologetic purpose that they had in their original position. There can be no question that the author was

concerned to make the point that the Baptist was not the preexistent logos, who is the subject of the hymn. What then is the connection between the Baptist and the logos? The answer we would suggest is that the logos Christology gives the full interpretation of Jesus (John 1:32) and the voice from heaven declaring Jesus to be the Son of God (John 1:34), that really meant that Jesus became at his baptism the incarnation of the preexistent Logos.

(3) The interpolation of verses 6–8, 15 also reinterprets the hymn itself. The shift from the *Logos asarkos* to the *ensarkos* now occurs not at verse 14 but earlier in the hymn. If R. Schnackenburg is right in regarding verse 5 as an addition of the Evangelist, this verse may already refer to the reception accorded to the incarnate Logos. But in any case, verse 9 must now refer to the *Logos ensarkos*, especially if, with Schnackenburg, we take "coming into the world" as an addition of the Evangelist's and as a predicate of the sentence rather than as an attribute of "every man." The coming of the light into the world takes place at Jesus' baptism. That verses 9–11 now refer to the incarnate logos is clinched by the Evangelist's further addition of verses 12–13, which speak of the inauguration of the community of faith, the Christian Church, as the result of the revelation of the Logos.[21] A further result of the Baptist interpolations is that the climactic assertion in verse 14, "the Word became flesh," will now refer not only to the Christ event in its totality (though that wider meaning is not entirely excluded), but specifically to the moment of Jesus' baptism.

This, of course, is a different Christology from that of the Nicene Creed, which linked the incarnation with Jesus' conception. But the nativity stories also express a different Christology from that of the Nicene Creed, for as recent exegesis has shown,[22] the infancy narratives know nothing of Christ's pre-existence. Rather, they are narrative expressions of the early kerygmatic affirmation of Jesus' Davidic descent as a qualification for his Messiahship.[23] Yet despite the difference between the Christologies of the Matthean and Lucan infancy narratives on the one hand, and the Johannine Prologue on the other, it is possible to build a bridge between them. Although the Fourth Gospel does not include an infancy narrative as such, Jesus is once made to refer to his birth: "For this was I born and for this I have come into the world, to bear witness to the truth" (John 18:37).[24] Thus the human birth of Jesus in the perspective of the Fourth Gospel, while not the moment of the incarnation, was nevertheless the beginning of Jesus' preparation for his unique role in salvation history. He was born to become the witness to the truth, that is, to incarnate in his witness the pre-existent Logos. We can link this interpretation of Jesus' birth with the Lucan references to the growth of Jesus from his infancy to his public ministry: "The child grew and became strong, *filled with wisdom*" (Luke 2:40). And a little later: "Jesus *increased in wisdom and in stature*" (Luke 2:50).

Furthermore, the history of Jesus from the moment of his birth or even, as the annunciation stories in Matthew and Luke make clear, from the moment of his virginal-pneumatic conception, was a history inaugurated by God himself. God by a direct creative intervention raised up the man Jesus and prepared him for the moment when at his baptism he should fulfill his eschatological role, a role which the Fourth Evangelist interprets as the enfleshment of the pre-existent Logos. The virginal conception and the infancy stories, together with John 18:37, secure the New Testament Christology against adoptionism. For adoptionism is a denial of the divine initiative. By taking the Johannine and synoptic Christologies together in this way, we are not seeking a false harmonization of the data, but seeking rather to do justice to the full witness of the New Testament canon.

The infancy narratives are rightly seen as a *Vorgeschichte;* they are not the *Geschichte* proper. The incarnation does not mean that the static qualities of divinity and humanity were somehow fused in a single person from the moment of his conception. That was a later interpretation in different categories. It means that God raised up a man who was at each stage of his historical growth being perfectly prepared to incarnate the divine logos in his human history. At each point of his ministry, Jesus in his humanity was a perfect instrument for his role. That human history did not emerge out of the ongoing flow of human history, but from God's intervention in that flow.

Christmas or Epiphany, which is the more important festival? The New Testament agrees with Eastern Orthodoxy and with Edward West that it was the baptism of Jesus rather than his birth that is of primary christological significance. Yet Christmas retains an importance of its own, for it marks the divinely initiated inauguration of the *Vorgeschichte*, a preparatory history to the real history. But the preparatory history, like the real history, is part of God's eschatological action, and as such, deserving of Christian celebration. While it would be more appropriate to read the Johannine Prologue in the Epiphany season as a comment on Jesus' baptism, we will doubtless go on reading it on Christmas Day. And when we hear the words, "The Word became flesh and dwelt among us, and we beheld his glory," we must remember that they are speaking not merely of what happened at Bethlehem, but of the whole history of Jesus of Nazareth to which Bethlehem was but a prelude.

NOTES

1. "The Incarnation in Historical Perspective," to appear in the *ATR*, Spring 1976. The thesis of that article begins with Jesus' prayer at John 11:41. Following Bultmann, I take this to mean that Jesus lived in constant prayer to the Father, and that through this prayer he constantly heard and responded to the call of the Father. As a result, his words became the Father's words and his works the Father's work. This call-and-response pattern in Jesus' life was initiated at his baptism. In this act, Jesus received his mission: he was "sent"

by the Father. All this is historical language. This historical language is complemented by another kind of language, derived from Jewish wisdom speculation. As the one sent by the Father in his baptism, Jesus incarnates the pre-existent heavenly wisdom—he is the light, the bread from heaven, etc., etc. The two levels of language may cross over one another, resulting in a sort of *communicatio ideomatum.* Thus Jesus can say, "I came down from heaven," or "Before Abraham was, I am"—not meaning that he is all this in his human person. But that it is the heavenly wisdom which he incarnates that is all this.

2. John 1:29–36. The Fourth Evangelist does not directly narrate the actual baptism of Jesus. He may have omitted it because of his anti-"baptist" polemic, for which see below. But 1:32 is obviously drawn from the baptismal narrative (descent of the Spirit) and so is verse 34, (the voice from heaven).

3. R. Bultmann, *The Gospel of John,* tr. G. R. Beasley-Murray *et al.* (Philadelphia: Westminster, 1971), 13073, esp. pp. 14–18.

4. C. Colpe, *Die Religionsgeschichtliche Schule* (FRLANT n.F.60; Göttingen: Vandenhoeck & Ruprecht, 1961). For a summary of Colpe and other authors, see W. Meeks, *The Prophet King* (Leiden: Brill, 1967), pp. 14–17.

5. E.g., E. Haenchen, "Probleme des johanneischen Prologs," *ZThK* 60 (1963), pp. 305–48; R. Schnackenburg, "Logos-Hymnus und johanneischer Prolog," *BZ,* n.F. 1 (1957), pp. 69–109, esp. pp. 96–101; James M. Robinson, "The Johannine Trajectory," in J. M. Robinson and H. Koester, *Trajectories Through Early Christianity* (Philadelphia: Fortress, 1971), pp. 232–68, esp. pp. 260–66.

6. R. Schnackenburg, "Logos-Hymnus," pp. 84–85. Cf. *idem, The Gospel According to St. John,* Vol, 1 (New York: Herder, 1968), p. 22. Schnackenburg's reconstruction is based on the two criteria of style-criticism and poetic form. Note that there are four stanzas, the first and the last with six lines, the second and the third with four lines. Other reconstructions have been proposed since Bultmann, notably E. Käsemann, "The Structure and Purpose of the Prologue to John's Gospel," *New Testament Questions of Today* (Philadelphia: Fortress, 1969), pp. 138–67, who proposes 1, (2), 3–5, (9), 10–12; E. Haenchen, "Probleme," who proposes 1–5, 9–11, 14, 16–17. British scholars are often characteristically cautious about the Prologue's hymnic origin, e.g., C. K. Barrett, *The Gospel According to St. John* (London: SPCK, 1955), pp. 125–26; M. D. Hooker, "John the Baptist and the Johannine Prologue," *NTS* 16 (1969–70), pp. 354–58. It is easy to stand on the sidelines and laugh at the lack of agreement over the extent of the original hymn, but fruitful exegesis demands that we take risks.

7. Blass–Debrunner–Funk, p. 332; a complexive (or constative) aorist is "used for linear actions which [having been accomplished] are regarded as whole."

8. See Schnackenburg, "Logos-Hymnus," p. 79. He compares vs. 12 (participle πιστεύουσιν in apposition to the pronoun αὐτοῖς) with 1 John 5:13. Typically Johannine are the expressions ἐις τὸ ὄνομα and τέκνα γενέσθαι recalls γεννηθῇ ἄνωθεν (John 3:3–5). The Moses/Christ comparison is Johannine (John 6:26ff.). By means of style-criticism, Schnackenburg assigns to the evangelist vss. 2,5,6–8, 12–13, 14b, c, and 16 ("Logos Hymnus," pp. 78–80).

9. C. Masson, "Le prologue du quatrième évangile," *RThPh,* N.s.28 (1940), pp. 297–311. R. E. Brown, *The Gospel According to John* (Anchor Bible 29; Garden City, N.Y.: Doubleday, 1966), p. 22, regards Masson's proposal with favor, except that he assigns the addition of the prologue to the later redactor.

10. Masson notes that this suggestion was anticipated by others, including R. Spitta and E. Hennecke ("Le prologue," p. 309). Bultmann dismisses this

Christmas, Epiphany, and the Johannine Prologue

view, citing Spitta as *"recht abenteuerlich,"* rendered in the E.T. "fantastic"—
which is, however, not the same thing (*John* 16,n. 6).

   11. It is interesting that the Trial Lectionary appoints John 1:6–8, 19–28 for
3 Advent B. Only vs. 15 is missing!

   12. μαρτυρία: 12 occurences outside the Prologue; μαρτυρεῖν 30 occurences.

   13. φῶς: 7 occurences outside the Prologue.

   14. The Johannine occurrences of πιστεύειν occupy two full columns in
Moulton and Gedden.

   15. Preexistence of the reality incarnate in Jesus is asserted or implied at 3:13;
6:36, 38, 41, 51a, 62; 13:3; 16:28, 17:5, 24. I have argued elsewhere ("The Incarnation
in Historical Perspective") that this does not mean the personal preexistence
of Jesus in his humanity but of the divine wisdom, equated with the Son of
man at 3:13 and 6:62. Where Jesus appears to speak of his preexistence, he does
so by a *communicatio idiomatum.*

   16. See above, note 3.

   17. John 1:19–42. (John is not the Messiah; true followers of the Baptist switch
to Jesus); 3:25–30 (Jesus is superior to the Baptist).

   18. Haenchen, "Probleme," p. 326.

   19. Luke 3:1–2. Opinions are divided as to whether this is Lucan composition,
the beginning of proto-Luke or the beginning of the Baptist's preaching in the
Lucan Special Material. My preference is not for the third possibility.

   20. Hooker, "John the Baptist," denies the presence of apologetic in favor
of a purely positive motive. This is difficult in view of vs. 8 and the sustained
apologetic later in the chapter.

   21. Vs. 5 may be intended by the Evangelist already to refer to the logos
ensarkos (so Käsemann and Schnackenburg). Schnackenburg (104) notes the
present θαίνει which, he holds, includes the post-Easter kerygma in the shin-
ing of the "light." Otherwise Haenchen, "Probleme," p. 320.

   22. R. Bultmann, "New Testament and Mythology" in H. W. Bartsch (ed.),
Kerygma and Myth I (London: SPCK, 1953), pp. 1–44, esp. p. 34. Cf. J. A. T.
Robinson, *The Human Face of God* (London: SCM, 1973), pp. 45–46.

   23. The virginal conception appears to be a later christological expression
inconsistent with Jesus' Davidic descent. Yet both Matthew and Luke com-
bine the two Christologies.

   24. There is also a discussion about the Messiah's birth at Bethlehem (John
7:41–42). But the Evangelist takes no position on the matter.

5

Maximus Confessor:

An Introduction

William B. Green

MAXIMUS called the Confessor (ca., A.D. 580–662) has been variously "acclaimed as 'the most universal spirit of the seventh century . . . probably the only productive thinker of his era . . . the real father of Byzantine theology . . . and perhaps the last independent thinker among the theologians of the Byzantine church.' "[1] To refer to Maximus as a "productive, independent thinker" can be highly misleading. For the very title of "confessor" implied, as has been observed, ". . . anything but being independent, original, or productive. . . ."[2] As confessor and theologian, Maximus was required to preserve, protect and defend orthodox Christian doctrine as it had been set down in Scripture, formulated by the Church Fathers, and codified by the Councils. The one thing upon which both sides in every controversy could agree, and in this Maximus was no exception, was that Scripture properly (i.e., spiritually) interpreted by the inspired and holy Fathers in harmony with one another constituted "the law and canon of the church."[3] Because the one whom we honor has in his own special way combined fidelity to tradition with theological creativity, the theology of Maximus Confessor seems an appropriate subject for consideration.

Allowing for his fundamental adherence to patristic authority, one may still find in the theology of Maximus a creative synthesis which served ". . . as a framework for the entire development of Byzantine Christian thought until the fall of Constantinople to the Turks."[4] The mystical tradition which he formulated and transmitted had a decisive influence upon such spiritual giants as Symeon the New Theologian and Gregory Palamas. His opposition to Hellenism on such issues as creation and freedom, his correction of the errors of Origenism and his transformation of its spirituality, his defense of Chalcedonian Christology presupposing the doctrine of "two-wills," his development of a specifically Christian cosmology and anthropology in which man is both microcosm and mediator, his identification of the knowledge of God with deification, his insistence on the universality of salvation and recapitulation—these are representative of Maximus' contributions to Byzantine theology.

It is impossible within the space of so brief an introduction to develop all of these topics. The ideas discussed in this paper are limited to the categories of anthropology and Christology. Under the heading of anthropology, we shall consider Maximus' views regarding man's original nature and state and Adam's fall—its causes and consequences. Under the heading of Christology, we shall examine the Maximian doctrine of the work of Christ, the two natures of Christ and finally the doctrine of deification, in which his anthropology and Christology come together.

Sources in English, both primary and secondary, for the study of Maximus are relatively few. Fr. Polycarp Sherwood translated *The Ascetic Life* and *The Four Centuries on Charity* and prefaced them with a general introduction to Maximian thought.[5] He also produced a chronology of Maximus' life and works along with a rejection of von Balthasar's thesis regarding an Origenistic crisis in Maximus' life.[6] Later Sherwood published a study of the *Ambigua* in which he vigorously refuted what some claimed to be Maximus' Origenism.[7] Recently Lars Thunberg argued the thesis that Maximus' anthropology provides the key to his theology as a whole.[8]

Apart from these special studies, Maximus has been treated by English writers largely in the context of historical studies[9] or in essays on Christology.[10] Most of these works are of relatively recent date.

The scarcity of English sources may account in some measure for the unfamiliarity with Maximus on the part of most students of theology in the West and may justify this attempt at a concise introduction. The writer's indebtedness to Sherwood and Thunberg will be obvious. However, an attempt has been made to avoid the elements of scholasticism in Sherwood's interpretation as well as the technological debates in Thunberg's comprehensive study.

Before proceeding to an examination of Maximus' thought, account must be taken of some of the major events in his life.

Maximus was born around A.D. 580 in Constantinople of an illustrious family and in a devout home. He received a superior education, with special emphasis on the study of philosophy. At that time, philosophical studies included arithmetic, music, geometry and astronomy as well as pure philosophy itself. The latter concentrated on the works of Plato and Aristotle, and the commentaries of Proclus and Iamblichus.

Because of his remarkable advancement in both virtue and learning, Maximus, at the age of thirty, was made first secretary to the Emperor Heraclius. His biographer tells that Maximus was gifted in realizing the demands of this situation, able to give good advice and to express his opinions readily. Hence, he made a profound impression on emperor and court.

After a relatively short time (c.613–14), Maximus left the court and entered the monastery of Chrysopolis, on the Asiatic shore opposite Constantinople. It is said that this move was prompted by his longing for a life of solitude (*καθ᾿ ἡσυχίαν*).

There he made exceptional progress in ascetic practices and devotional life, impressing his fellow monks by his religious zeal. The length of his stay at Chrysopolis is not known. His departure is thought to have been prompted by the Persian invasions of 626.

After stops in Crete and Cyprus, Maximus arrived in Carthage (c.630). During his early years in Africa, Maximus composed two major works: *Questions to Thalassius*[11] and the first of the two *Ambigua.*[12] He stayed in a monastery called Eucratas, which had for its abbot Sophronius, the first to fight the monothelite heresy, and the person responsible for alerting Maximus to its dangers. Maximus himself became deeply involved in the monothelite controversies from about 634 until his death in 662. His opposition to monothelitism (or monoenergism) was sparked by the *Ecthesis* of 638, a document promulgated over the emperor's signature which contained an injunction to " '. . . confess one will of Our Lord and true God Jesus Christ,' that there be no chance of conflict between the human nature and the divine Word."[13]

Pope Theodore (consecrated November 24, 642) took note of the *Ecthesis*, which he thought to be the work of Pyrrhus (deposed patriarch of Constantinople), and insisted that he be sent by the emperor to Rome. Maximus was in full accord with the papal action, writing at length to Peter the Illustrious against Pyrrhus and the monothelite heresy. When Pyrrhus took refuge in Africa, Maximus resumed the dispute which eventually resulted in Pyrrhus' return to orthodoxy and his recognition as patriarch by the Pope.

After the disputation, Maximus left Africa for Rome, traveling with or arriving about the same time as Pyrrhus. The latter did not remain long in or faithful to Rome. When Pyrrhus reverted to monothelitism, he was excommunicated by Pope Theodore. Meanwhile in Constantinople, Pyrrhus was reintroduced as patriarch, thus completing the break with Rome.

Remaining in Rome, Maximus began a period of intense activity in defense of orthodoxy. He composed a tome (florilegia) to Stephen of Dora against the *Ecthesis*. This tome contains twenty-nine citations from the Fathers relating to the question in dispute. He also formulated the doctrine of the two wills and operations of Christ.

Inspired by Maximus, the new Pope, Martin I, summoned a Lateran Council in 649, at which Maximus was probably present. This council condemned the monothelite heresy and stipulated punishment to those who advocated it. These decisions were circulated throughout the Christian world. Constans II, the Emperor, reacted at once. He sent the Exarch of Ravenna to Rome to force acceptance of the *Typos*, which forbade controversy for or against "one will in Christ." But the Exarch defected. The Emperor could do nothing until after the Exarch's death, when he had both the Pope and Maximus arrested and brought back to Constantinople. The Pope was tried in 654 and was sent into exile. Maximus did not come to trial until May of 655. Every effort was made to charge him with political crimes for his refusal to communicate with the see of Constantinople as long as she acknowledged the *Typos* of Constans. These efforts failed, however, as did those to persuade Maximus to change his mind. Hence Maximus was sent into temporary exile at Bizya in Thrace. After further attempts to persuade him to surrender to the Emperor's will, i.e., adhere to the *Typos*, also failed, he was sent a second time into exile at Perberis, also in Thrace, where he remained for six years.

In 662, Maximus and two of his disciples were brought back to Constantinople for another definitive council. There Maximus and the two Anastasius' (his disciples) were anathematized and turned over to civil officers for punishment: the mutilation of those members by which they had propounded the doctrine of two wills. Their tongues and right hands were amputated. Then they were exposed to public ridicule before being sent to exile in Lazica, on the southeast shore of the Black Sea. Maximus, broken with age and abusive treatment, died there on the 13th of August of the same year (662).[14]

Anthropology

MAN'S NATURE AND PLACE

In Maximian thought, men, like every created thing, were made according to their particular *logoi* which pre-exist in God from all eternity. These *logoi* are God's ideas ("thought-wills") about beings. They are the Divine Intentions which are given substance and existence in creation. The *logoi* have their center in and are expressions of the Divine *logos*, the second person of the Trinity, Who is both the first principle and the last end of all creatures, as well as the One in Whom the differentiated *logoi* are held together. One who has the wisdom will see, said Maximus, ". . . both the one *logos* as many *logoi*, and the many *logoi* as the one *logos.*" It is in this manner that the *logoi* present in creation represent an incarnation of the Divine.[15]

Man was not only created according to the *logos*, but also bears the image of the Divine *logos*. Thus he is endowed with a natural tendency toward God which makes of him not an autonomous being, but one whose true nature is realized only insofar as he exists or participates in God. This condition of "natural participation" is, according to Maximus, both a gift and a task. That is to say, man is called to realize by his personal act of free choice that divine potential with which he was endowed.

In bringing into being persons endowed with reason and understanding, God, in Maximus' view, communicated to them four of the divine attributes by which He maintains, guards, and preserves beings: being, ever-being (or eternity), goodness and wisdom. The first two belong to man as a creature made in God's image: first, in the image of His being, by the fact of being; secondly, in the image of His ever-being, by the fact of being always, if not without beginning, at least without end. The second two, goodness and wisdom, pertain to the resemblance or likeness of God, and are attributed to man's free choice. Consequently, every reasonable nature is in the image of God; but only those who are good and wise are in His likeness.[16]

Man occupies furthermore a special place in the created order, as the one in whom the two spheres of the universe— the intelligible and the sensible—are united. "For all things which have been created by God, in their diverse natures, are brought together in man as in a melting pot, and form in him," declares Maximus, "one unique perfection—a harmony composed of many different notes."[17] This union is analogous to the hypostatic union of the two natures in Christ. Just as Christ unites within Himself the human and divine natures, so man forms within himself the unity of created natures. In both instances, this union is hypostatic.

Man's middle position between the extremes of creation carries with it a special task. In Maximian thought, it was the original destiny of man to order and unify the whole creation, beginning with himself, on the basis of his own harmonious relationship with God. He was intended to transform the world into paradise, and to reconcile[18] heaven and earth, the intelligible and sensible, man and woman, God and His creation.[19] This having been accomplished, man was to abandon himself completely to God, thereby returning the whole of creation knit together in his own being. Then God would give Himself to man, who by virtue of this gift, that is by grace, would become all that God Himself is by nature. Thus the deification of man and universe would be complete.[20]

IMAGE AND LIKENESS

Reference has already been made to the Maximian distinction between image and likeness. But more needs to be said on that subject. As far as is known, Irenaeus was the first Christian writer to employ that distinction. He reckoned image to be related to nature as such, body as well as soul, and incapable of being lost. Likeness he thought to be an addition, given through Adam, destroyed by the fall, but restored by Christ. Irenaeus equated likeness with the presence of the Spirit in man's soul.[21]

Maximus' use of this distinction follows the Alexandrian tradition, developed by Clement and Origen. Origen maintained that the image of God was given to man in the beginning, but that the likeness is to be acquired through a spiritual process, i.e., by imitation of God and by manifestation of divine virtues. The key Maximian text reads as follows: "They say that God and man are exemplars one of another; and that God makes himself man for man's sake out of love, so far as man, enabled by God through charity, deified himself; and that man is rapt up by God in mind to the unknowable, so far as man has manifested through virtues the God by nature invisible."[22]

In the above passage the reciprocity between God and man, a characteristic feature of Maximus' theology, is offered as an explanation of the fact that man in deification bears the image of God in perfection. The development of man's image character is an expression of a divine-human reciprocity in function, in which man moves entirely toward God and is more and more established in Him through the contemplative motion of his mind. At the same time, God becomes incarnate in man through human virtues which reflect divine attributes. Human establishment in God and divine incarnation through human virtues are two aspects of the same process of deification. It appears that Maximus adopted the old distinction between image and likeness in order to show the reciprocity of God and man, as well as the different aspects of God's activity toward created rational beings.[23]

In Maximus, man's image character is closely connected with his rational nature and his mind ($\nu o \hat{v} \varsigma$), and is balanced by an emphasis on human freedom. Dominion over irrational creation is also an expression of the image character of man. The body, too, is involved, although not in the localization of the image, but in its realization.

Likeness, on the other hand, is consistently linked by Maximus to the "life of virtues," the *vita practica*. Activity is associated with likeness, as contemplation is with image. While self-determination as such belongs to the image character, its true development discloses the likeness to God. To what is naturally good through the image, man by his free decision must add a likeness through virtues. Likeness thus perfects the image character of man in that it completes what is of nature. The appropriation of the divine virtues is also a formation of Christ in the believer, an individual appropriation of the presence of the incarnate λόγος.[24]

THE WILL

Basic to the Maximian understanding of human nature are his concepts of freedom and will. Although not identical, the two are closely related. The power of self-determination, which is the expression of man's uniqueness and pertains to the divine image, ". . . is a willing of the rational soul, tending without let to whatever it wants."[25] Self-determination, freedom, willing imply self-movement. Hence Maximus identifies will and energy. "Energy is life in general; will is the life of the spirit, i.e., a particularized energy."[26] That is to say, will is the energy or activity appropriate to intelligent nature. It is the power by which the rational subject expresses its relationship to others, to the cosmos and to God. The use to which this energy is put, the form which this activity takes, depends upon the spiritual subject, the νοῦς.

To illustrate the function of the will, Maximus employs the analogy of a plant. The growth of a plant is a highly structured activity, directed by the λόγοι of plant life, and its place in God's creative scheme. Likewise in the case of man. The movement to which man is ordained and the role of the λόγοι in the basic structure of his nature provide a definite direction for the human will. Man is called to a certain growth (deification), and his will is the energy by which that growth occurs. While the λόγοι of creation give man's will a sense of direction; the will, in turn, gives man's life movement. Without this willful energy, man would be static, incapable of movement, of striving toward God.

Thus the connection between will and freedom is made explicit. The will is the vehicle for freedom, the power which makes possible self-determination. The natural will has a Godward tendency which, when fulfilled, increases man's freedom. But again, the will is merely instrumental to freedom. It allows man to be free by enabling him to move toward God.

It is important, in connection with the will, to examine the Maximian concept of *gnome* (γνώμη). In his early works, Maximus appears "to use the term *gnome* in a sense almost synonymous with 'will' or 'energy,' and some passages . . . seem to admit the existence of a divine *gnome*. Later, and very clearly, *gnome* becomes the main term to designate the free will of created hypostases, the seat of the 'posse peccare' (potential sin.)"[27]

As the latter, *gnome* is the center in man which decides for or against his natural inclination toward God. This implies choice, and choice implies knowledge. Sherwood notes that the root of γνώμη is γνο, which infers knowledge; but that Maximus' usage points to a meaning akin to will. Accordingly, one may conclude that for Maximus γνώμη is a (hypostatic) will of discernment.[28] Just as nature moves according to its will, which is defined by its inner structure, so the hypostasis moves according to its *gnome*, i.e., toward what it has discerned to be a desirable object. Thus the hypostasis functions according to a dynamic exactly analogous to that of the natural will.

This understanding of *gnome* explains Maximus' willingness in his early writings to attribute *gnome* to Christ, with the provision, of course, that in Him it was without passions and in perfect accord with nature. His later insistence on only one hypostasis (the divine) in Christ, excluded the possibility of *gnome*, since *gnome* is a function of the created hypostasis, and in Christ there was no human hypostasis.

Eventually, Maximus recognized an intimate relation between *gnome* and sin, a further reason for its denial to Christ. The battleground of the first temptation, the target of the Devil's attack, was Adam's *gnome*. And the immediate consequence of his sin was the contamination of his *gnome*. "Man acquired in this way a *gnomic* will, which chooses, hesitates, ignores the real good, inflicts pain because its decisions are taken blindfolded; it is 'a kind of desire adhering to what is, or what he thinks is, a relative good.' "[29]

MAN'S ORIGINAL STATE

As to man's original state, Maximus maintains that Adam possessed spiritual freedom which he exercised in communion with God. He had the capacity for spiritual pleasure; was without sin; was free of physical corruption and was subject only to the law of "coming into being," not to that of physical birth. For sexual intercourse was introduced only after the fall as a means of procreation and the counterpart of death. In elaboration of the Genesis statement that the first man was naked, Maximus says, ". . . Adam was naked, not in the sense that he was without flesh or body, but to the extent that he was free from that which makes the human flesh heavier, mortal and resistant. He could live without the aid of any human technique and without any clothes, since he had detachment and thus had no need to have shame, and further was not subject to any extreme of cold or heat. He was passionless by grace, free from needs caused by outward circumstances, and wise, since he enjoyed knowledge above the sphere of purely natural contemplation."[30]

THE FALL: ITS CAUSES AND CONSEQUENCES

Maximus' views on Adam's fall, its causes and consequences, are in agreement with those of earlier Greek Fathers,
and may be summarized as follows: Sin is the fault, not of God,
but of man. Its causes are to be found in man's misuse of his
freedom and in the devil's seduction. The devil, whose fall is
attributable to pride, desired that man share his fall, concealed
his jealousy with benevolence and persuaded man to set his
affection on things other than the Cause of all, thereby produc-
ing in him ignorance of this cause. Yet the fall was entirely
man's fault. For he allowed himself to be persuaded to direct
his capacity for pleasure toward the sensible world, preferring
its pleasures to God.[31]

However, sensual pleasure always involves a negative counterpart, pain—which in man's case is both punitive and purga-
tive. Thus he is started on a never-ending cycle in pursuit of
pleasure and escape from pain. Maximus depicts all of the
devastating consequences of man's fall as the result of the
pleasure-pain dialectic. From pursuit of the one and avoidance
of the other, all the passions arise.[32]

The physical aspect of man's life becomes marked by pleasure and pain, which in turn introduces a law of death designed
to terminate his escape from his natural goal. Death is, therefore, the culmination of pain. Note that it is the sting of sin
(death), not sin itself and guilt, which is transmitted to suc-
ceeding generations. Guilt belongs to the *gnome*, to the hypostasis, and hence to each particular person. Only the dislocation
and disorientation which is the result of original sin is passed
along, and which, in turn, makes our personal sin unavoidable.
The notion of inherited guilt is altogether foreign to both
Maximian and Byzantine thought.

A second consequence is the introduction of the law of
procreation through conception and birth. So man gains life
by that very lust which is a prime example of sensual pleasure.[33] But this does not mean, as far as Maximus is concerned,
that marriage and the act of generation are sinful. Marriage

may, in fact, be good, and the sexual act well used. Yet the condition of mankind which requires its use is one of the consequences of sin.[34]

Thirdly, man experiences that the sensible world cannot satisfy his desire, and that by trying to make corruptible things permanent, he increases their corruptibility. Yet he cannot avoid searching for fulfillment in that world. His choice has become his curse.[35]

Finally, fallen man suffers, according to Maximus, from three fundamental evils: ignorance, self-love and tyranny, each of which depends upon and sustains the other. Ignorance refers to lack of knowledge of God as the cause of all good things and implies failure to move toward virtue. Ignorance increases self-love, which is the root of all passions including bodily lust and human pride. "Passion is a movement of the soul contrary to nature, either in irrational love, or in senseless hate . . . or on account of some material thing."[36] "The origin of all the passions is self-love, and their end, pride."[37] Self-love leads to tyranny, both of the individual through passion, and against other human beings through divisive and destructive actions. "These passions then bind the mind to the material things and hold it down to earth, lying upon them like a massive stone, whereas by nature it is lighter and more agile than fire."[38] When love for God is turned in upon the self, love for the neighbor becomes impossible.

It is significant that in the Maximian view, human nature remains uncorrupted in spite of sin. This explains why the Word could assume human nature, without sin. It was the capacity for self-determination, the *gnomic* will, which went astray and became perverted. "But ours [will] is manifestly merely human and in no way impeccable, because of its deviation to this side or that. This is not to say that nature is altered," declares Maximus, "but that the movement has deviated; or to speak more truthfully, that the nature has changed its mode. This is manifest from the fact that the nature does many things irrationally, yet its substance from its inherent rationality never passes over into something irrational."[39]

Christology

Having examined the Maximian doctrine of man's nature, including his original and actual condition, we may now consider his ideas on deification and the work of Christ. Man's becoming God is seen by Maximus only as the result of God's becoming man. Hence, the mystery of Christ stands, as Sherwood claims, at the very center of the Maximian system.[40]

THE WORK OF CHRIST

The work of Christ for Maximus, as for Irenaeus, is conceived as recapitulation. The One by Whom and in Whom all things were created in the beginning restores and integrates the whole of creation by assuming it Himself. The consequences of Adam's act are taken away by Christ's act, and in Him man's true destiny, as predetermined by God, is achieved.

Man is thereby liberated from the laws which constitute his collective imprisonment. Through Christ's birth without carnal pleasure, i.e., His birth from a Virgin, the law of lust was overcome. Through His voluntary death without sin, the law of death was transformed from a judgment of death into a condemnation of sin. Through the ascension and exaltation of the human body, consubstantial with ours, heaven and earth are reunited. By transcending the angelic order with his human body and soul, the unity of sense and mind is restored, and the harmony of all creation is reestablished.[41] In sum, through Christ, man's destiny and God's purpose, i.e., deification, are fulfilled. This Maximus describes as follows: ". . . that whole people might participate in the whole God, and that in the same way in which the soul and the body are united, God should become accessible for participation by the soul and, through the soul's intermediary, by the body, in order that the soul might receive an unchanging character and the body, immortality; and finally that the whole man should become God, deified by the grace of God-become-man, becoming whole man, soul and body, by nature, and becoming whole God, soul and body, by grace."[42]

Maximus is one of the few ancients to consider whether there would have been an Incarnation if there had not been a Fall. If, as Maximus claims, the recapitulation of all things in Christ is in fact the true end of creation, then it must follow, as Maximus also claims, that the Incarnation was foreseen and foreordained quite apart from man's destructive misuse of his freedom. This view is consistent with Maximus' notion of created nature as a dynamic process directed toward an eschatological goal, which is Christ the incarnate Logos.[43]

THE TWO NATURES

Maximus' principal contribution in the area of Christology was his formulation of the doctrine of the two wills in Christ. The doctrine of two natures affirmed by the Council of Chalcedon (451) presupposed, even necessitated, according to Maximus, the doctrine of two wills or energies. Nature, as Aristotle had defined it and Maximus understood it, requires movement, and movement requires energy. Without will or energy, there can be no movement, and without movement, no nature. If, as Chalcedon insisted, there were two natures in Christ, there had to be two wills. There simply cannot be true divinity without a divine will, or true humanity without a human will, or two authentic natures—one divine and one human—without two wills. Such was Maximus' chief argument against the Monothelites (or Monoenergists), who maintained that Christ's humanity had lost its human will (or energy) owing to its union with divinity.[44]

Maximus defends the two natures of Christ on at least three other grounds. His consubstantiality with us in our humanity assumes a human will which is not superseded by His divine will. Furthermore, the work of Christ as recapitulation requires a human will. At this point, Maximus employs the axiom of Gregory of Nazianzus, "What is not assumed is not healed, and what is united to God is saved,"[45] to argue that man's salvation depends upon the incarnate Christ's having a distinct human will. Otherwise that aspect which bears both the blame and the consequences of the fall remains unrestored.

In addition to the foregoing anthropological, Christological and soteriological considerations, there was a fundamental theological concern which necessitated the two natures doctrine. Participation, which was the key to the Maximian understanding of life in God, requires the presence of the divine will in Christ. Otherwise, the invisible, inaccessible God has not become visible and accessible.

DEIFICATION

The concluding topic is the Maximian doctrine of deification which may be regarded as ". . . a summary of his whole theological anthropology."[46] Deification is the fulfillment of man's capacity for God. In deification, man becomes by grace, i.e., through participation in the Divine energies, what God is by nature.[47]

Hence for Maximus, deification is identical with redemption. It was instituted by God, and accomplished by "the Lord's becoming man." As the old man explains to the brother in *The Ascetic Life:* "Taking flesh by the Holy Spirit and the holy Virgin, He showed us a godlike way of life; He gave us holy commandments and promised the kingdom of heaven to those who lived according to them . . . Suffering His saving Passion and rising from the dead, He bestowed upon us the hope of resurrection and of eternal life. From the condemnation of ancestral sin, He absolved by obedience; by death He destroyed the power of death . . . Then, ascended into heaven and seated on the right of the Father, He sent the Holy Spirit as a pledge of life, and as enlightenment and sanctification for our souls, and as a help to those who struggle to keep His commandments for their salvation. This, in brief, is the purpose of the Lord's becoming man."[48]

But deification also depends upon man's renewed powers. To right faith, the Lord joined, asserted Maximus, "the keeping of all the commandments. He knew that one, apart from the other, was not able to save man."[49] But who can keep all the commandments? "He who imitates the Lord and follows in His footsteps." Salvation or deification is thus a matter of faith *and* works, grace *and* free will. "See the Lord bestowed on us the method of salvation," declared Maximus, "and has given us eternal power to become sons of God. So finally then our salvation is in our will's grasp."[50]

Yet this dependence on the will does not exclude but presupposes grace. Through grace one receives faith, then the power to imitate Christ and to follow his commandments. By the same grace man's powers are renewed so that, separating himself from worldly things, he is able to lead an ascetical life and to love both God and his neighbor, which is the fulfillment of every commandment. The fullest effect of man's deification is in love whereby he comes nearest to the imitation of Christ. ". . . any ascetic life or practice that is without love is," in Maximus' view, "a stranger to God."[51]

Given the primacy of the *gnome* in man's fall, the restoration of the *gnome* becomes a matter of first importance. This is accomplished by participation in, imitation of and union with Christ. But knowledge and love are also required: knowledge in order that the *gnome* can discern the good, and love in order that the *gnome* may remain fixed in it. Maximus describes three stages in the transformation of the *gnome:* the active life *(praxis),* the contemplative life *(theoria),* and theology *(theologia).* "The mind which follows well the active life advances in prudence, the contemplative life, in knowledge. To the one it belongs to bring the contender to a discernment of virtue and vice; to the other to lead the participant to the essences of the incorporeal and corporeal creation. Then, finally, it is fit for the grace of theology, when it has passed beyond, on the wings of charity, all the things just mentioned; and, being in God, it will examine through the Spirit, the essential concerning Him, as much as the human mind may."[52]

The goal of the first stage is detachment, to deliver man from his passions. This is accomplished by charity, prayer and self-control: "Check the soul's irascible element with charity; the concupiscible reduce with self-mastery; and wing its rational part with prayer."[53] All of this is aimed, obviously, at the restoration of the primal balance of man's nature. And this being restored, man is free once again to follow his natural inclination toward God. This first stage is considered a prerequisite for the second.

The goal of the second stage is knowledge of the essence of things and of God's activity in the world. Through contemplation, man comes to the *logoi* (principles) which are at the basis of all created things, and finally to the one primal *logos*. This is the path from creation to Creator, or what Dionysius called "cataphatic" theology. It leads to knowledge of the divine properties or energies, but not of the divine essence. One might describe this stage as one of penetration into the "epiphanic" quality of creation. It results in knowledge of God, which, in turn, generates love of God. The ignorance and blindness of the *gnome* are thus overcome, and man's intellectual vision restored.

The first two stages, which interpenetrate each other, are preparatory for the third, in which the Christian enters into *Theosis* (deification). Things, passions and their representation are transcended and man stands face to face with God, Who remains essentially unknowable even when one is united mystically to Him. This is the path of "apophatic" theology, the ecstasy of being taken up into the "cloud of unknowing," of being ravished by the divine beauty and love. It is the high point of participation, the consummation of the likeness, the achievement of deification. Maximus describes it as ". . . the whole man become God, deified by the grace of God-become-man, becoming the whole man, soul and body, by nature, and becoming the whole God, soul and body, by grace."[54]

The Maximian understanding of this final stage is profoundly influenced by Christology. This highest form of perfection, deification *(theosis)*, is a reflection of the hypostatic unity and interpenetration *(perichoresis)* of the divine and human in Christ. It is effected without any confusion or violation of natures, but with an expression of human and divine characteristics in communion with each other. Thus, Maximus links the doctrines of deification and incarnation. That is to say, the basis of man's deification is the hypostatic union of the divine and human in Christ. And the deifying effect of the incarnation is, in turn, grounded in God's original purpose for man, i.e., that he participate in the divine nature. Deification is accomplished by grace alone, according to Maximus, yet God becomes man insofar as man has deified himself, assuming, of course, that man has God as his natural desire. Hence, the incarnation of the Divine *logos* takes place in the believer, that is to say, in his virtues which themselves represent a revelatory movement of God toward man. The two, deification and incarnation, are reciprocal, the one being, for Maximus, the obverse of the other. Wherever incarnation occurs, deification also takes place, and vice versa.[55]

One may ask to what extent Maximus regards deification as simply a restoration to an original incorruption and immortality, or alternatively, as the development of mankind beyond Adam's primordial condition. For Maximus' predecessors, Origen and Evagrius, deification is a return to an original unity of all intelligible beings, whereas Gregory of Nyssa allows the possibility of spiritual development that transcends any primal state. It may be argued that the primitive state was not, in Maximus' view, a state of deification, but of order, i.e., "a perfection of the creature tending toward its ordained end."[56] Fullness of union had not yet been achieved. Man still needed to grow in love in order to realize the will of his Creator. Recognizing an element of fiction in every distinction between man's original state and that conferred by deification, as well as in every attempt to be explicit about the latter, it is still possible to interpret deification as a state of continuing perfection, of becoming according to God's will, of ever increasing participation in the divine energies. Maximus, following Gregory of Nyssa, claims that angelic nature is capable of unending development in good things but without temporal succession. He sees no reason to deny a similar growth according to its nature to every created thing. Such is the nature and extent of deification, according to Maximus.[57]

This, in very summary fashion, is the theology of Maximus Confessor. Many of the themes which are central to his teaching appear over and over again in the preaching and writing of Edward Nason West. Both share a common understanding of man's nature and destiny, as well as of God's energetic love, which provides for man's redemption. And both seek for that "perfect mind . . . which, by true faith, in supreme ignorance, knows the supremely Unknowable."[58]

NOTES

1. Jaroslav Pelikan, *The Spirit of Eastern Christendom* (Chicago: University of Chicago Press, 1974), (hereafter cited as *Spirit*), p.8.

2. *Ibid.*

3. *Ibid.*

4. John Meyendorff, *Byzantine Theology* (New York: Fordham University Press, 1974), p.3.

5. Polycarp Sherwood, trans., *St. Maximus the Confessor: The Ascetic Life* and the *Four Centuries on Charity*, Ancient Christian Writers; Vol. XXI (London: Longmans, Green and Co., 1955).

6. Polycarp Sherwood, "An Annotated Date-list of the Works of Maximus the Confessor," *Studia Anselmia*, Vol. XXX, (1952).

7. Polycarp Sherwood, "The Earlier Ambigua of St. Maximus the Confessor," *Studia Anselmia*, Vol. XXXVI, (1955).

8. Lars Thunberg, *Microcosm and Mediator* (Lund: Gleerup, 1965), (hereafter cited as *Microcosm*).

9. E.g., Meyendorff, *Byzantine Theology;* Pelikan, *Spirit;* and two works by

Maximus Confessor: An Introduction

Vladimir Lossky in translation: *The Mystical Theology of the Eastern Church* (Cambridge: James Clark and Co., Ltd., 1957) and *The Vision of God* (London: Faith Press, 1963).

10. E.g., John Meyendorff, *Christ in Eastern Christian Thought* (Washington: Corpus Books, 1969), (hereafter cited as *Christ*), pp. 99–115.

11. The *Questions* was addressed to a Libyan priest and monk, and contained sixty-five answers to scriptural problems solved by reference to patristic writings, particularly the works of Gregory of Nazianzus and the Pseudo-Dionysius.

12. *The Ambigua* was written at the request of Bishop John of Cyzicus to put down in writing the substance of their discussions over various difficult passages of Gregory the Theologian.

13. Sherwood, "Introduction" in *Ancient Christian Writers*, XXI (hereafter cited as "Introduction"), p. 18.

14. *Ibid.*, p. 27.

15. *Ibid.*, p. 46.

16. St. Maximus Confessor, *The Four Centuries on Charity*, trans. by Polycarp Sherwood, III, p. 24.

17. Quoted by Lossky, *Mystical Theology*, p. 108. Exact location not specified.

18. I.e., overcome the divisions *(διαιρέσις)* on the moral level, but not the differences *(διαφοραί)* on the ontological level.

19. This understanding of man's task does not imply that creation was defective initially, and that man was made at the last minute in order to bring together a fragmented creation. On the contrary, creation, in Maximus' view, takes place with man in mind, i.e., man as the keystone of the arch whose central position holds together opposing sides.

20. St. Maximus Confessor, *Ambigua*, 41; PG 91:1305D. Cf. Lossky, ibid., p. 109–10.

21. Thunberg, *Microcosm*, pp. 120–33.

22. *Ambigua* 10–113 B10-C2; Quoted by Sherwood, *The Early Ambigua*, p. 144.

23. Thunberg, *Microcosm*, pp. 134–35.

24. *Ibid.*, pp. 136–37.

25. Sherwood, "Introduction," p. 55.

26. Cf. V.V. Bolotov, *Lektsii po Istorii Drevneii Tserkvii* (Petrograd, 1918), IV, p. 473.

27. Myendorff, *Christ*, pp. 112–13.

28. Sherwood, "Introduction," pp. 58–60.

29. Myendorff, *Christ*, p. 113.

30. *Ambigua* 45; PG 91, 1353ABCD: summarized by Thunberg, *Microcosm*, p. 153.

31. According to Maximus, man's natural desire for God was diverted in the very first instant: " 'On his coming to be,' man gave himself up to sense and through sense to sense objects, so that his very first movement resulted in pleasure outside the scope of his nature, short of the scope of his nature." THAL 61, 628AB, quoted by Sherwood, *op. cit.*, p. 64.

32. Cf. Thunberg, *Microcosm*, pp. 164–69.

33. Thunberg, *Microcosm*, p. 169.

34. Sherwood, "Introduction," p. 55.

35. Thunberg, *Microcosm*, p. 170.

36. *Four Centuries*, II, p. 16.

37. *Ibid.*, III, p. 57.

38. *Ibid.*, p. 56.

39. Maximus Confessor, *Opuscula Theologica et Polemica*, 20, 236D; quoted by Sherwood, *Introduction*, pp. 56–57.

40. Sherwood, "Introduction," p. 29.

41. Maximus Confessor, *Ambigua* 41, 1304D-1316A; cf. Thunberg, *Microcosm*, p. 162.

42. Maximus Confessor, *Ambigua* 1088; quoted by Meyendorff, *Byzantine Theology*, p. 164.

43. Cf. Meyendorff, *Byzantine Theology*, p. 160–61.

44. Cf. Meyendorff, *Christ*, pp. 110–15; *Byzantine Theology*, pp. 133, 153, 185.

45. Gregory of Nazianzus, *Ad Cledonium*, PG 37, col. 181.

46. Thunberg, *Microcosm*, p. 457.

47. Or as Palamas, in thought borrowed from Maximus, was later to write: man "becomes by participation that which the Archetype is as cause." *Triads*, I, 3, 39.

48. St. Maximus the Confessor, *The Ascetic Life*, p. 103–04.

49. *Ibid.*, p. 104.

50. *Ibid.*, p. 133; cf. *The Four Centuries*, I, p. 39. This is suggested also by Maximus' development of the term "perichoresis" to refer to the reciprocal relationship between God and man. According to Maximus ". . . the incarnation of God and the deification of man condition each other mutually . . . Man becomes God as it were, in proportion to God's becoming man, and he is elevated for God's sake to the extent to which God has emptied himself, without change, and accepted human nature." Cf. Thunberg, *Microcosm*, p. 33. Maximus intends this formula to be an elaboration of the Christological insights of Chalcedon which affirms the union of two natures without confusion or change.

51. *Ibid.*, p. 125.

52. *The Four Centuries*, II, p. 26. Maximus follows Evagrius in his three stages of Christian development.

53. *The Four Centuries*, IV, p. 80.

54. Quoted by Meyendorff, *Christ*, p. 109.

55. Thunberg, *Microcosm*, pp. 451–57.

56. Lossky, *Mystical Theology*, p. 99.

57. *Ibid.*, pp. 101–03.

58. *Caritas* 3:99 (PG 90:1048).

6

The Visibility of Christ
and the Affliction of Transcendence

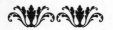

Alan W. Jones

"Aspicit eum cuius nomen est Oriens: He watches for him whose name is Light."[1] Thus John Donne's epitaph describes him. *Expectans expectavi:* "He is waiting with eager expectation for the Light." He was its disciple. He struggled with it, sought to manipulate it, was burned by it. In the end, he surrendered to it, finding it not the harbinger of death, but rather the bearer of life and love which is stronger than death.

Donne's first sermon as Dean of St. Paul's was delivered on Christmas Day, 1621, on the text: "He was not that light, but was sent to bear witness of that light" (John 1:8). His own life as a Christian and as a priest, like that of John the Baptist, pointed to the light of Christ. In the chaotic and disturbing world of the seventeenth century, such men were needed. It was a period of great personal and political disintegration. It was the death throes of what we call the Middle Ages. Donne heralded the coming of a new era, and he was made and scarred by the events which shaped him and his age. He knew what it was to live in a time of the dying of a culture, experiencing its painful and embarrassing rigor mortis. He also felt something of the pangs of new birth.

Donne is fascinating for us because his own person was the battleground of the forces of change struggling for control in his age. He assisted at the birth of what we call the modern world. Like us, he lived in a world that was dying. Like us, he sensed the birth tremors of a *novum*. This "new thing" was so present to him and in him that he was prepared to risk everything to help usher in the coming age. He lived during the birth of modern astronomy, which not only exploded the medieval cosmology but caused a profound upheaval in the human psyche, in man's self-understanding. The great literature of the time helped mankind to adjust. Shakespeare and Milton were able to describe the coming realities, using the terminology of the old cosmology. Donne, in his writing, took up the theological and personal issues surfacing as a result of Baconian science. Was not Christianity too provincial, too mundane, to cope with the emerging "brave new world"? Were not man's moral resources too weak to cope with seventeenth-century "future shock"? Donne's answer to these strangely contemporary questions was "No," even if the answer involved his own ruin. As Robert S. Jackson eloquently writes:

> In a world threatened with cleavages so severe as to seem to destroy it, some heroic effort to hold it together, even at the threat to personal bifurcation, seemed justified.[2]

Our world is thus threatened, and heroes are in short supply.

To read John Donne, particularly the Sermons, in the light of contemporary events, is an exhilarating experience. He is our contemporary as an apostle of light in dark times. Edward West, priest and friend, to whom this essay is dedicated, is also a man who "watches for him whose name is light." He manages to incarnate the best of Anglicanism. His preaching is in the Donne tradition, his theology Cappadocian, his spirituality Johannine. Edward West and John Donne are fellow spirits: they touch other lives in identical ways, by preaching and by waiting for the light. Edward West, in the spirit of Donne, of Gregory of Nyssa, of St. John the Evangelist, writes:

> To be alive, to be able to see, and to know where we are going—is there anything else which matters? Not if the words are properly defined! To know the only true God, and Jesus Christ whom he has sent, is to have life eternal starting right here and now. To know ourselves and each other as bearers of the image of God is to see what Jesus really means to the life of men—to know him as God's Word to us about ourselves.[3]

This paragraph eloquently describes John Donne's own longing and discontent. To live, to see, to know—these were the things which drove him mad. He was beside himself with erotic love, with ambition, and with despair. Finally he was driven into the arms of Christ in whom he found God's Word about himself. Christian or not, Donne was a man afflicted with that peculiarly human disease, transcendence. He was convinced that human beings carry around within them, at their deepest, a terrible "otherness" and that this otherness was forever calling them "to be," recreating them *ex nihilo*. Donne, then, was driven by the conviction that there is always more, that man was called continually to go beyond himself. His life, after his conversion, was to make this Christ visible, available, palpable to others. He came to see that transcendence was not so much an affliction as a terrible gift from a loving God.

Donne was born early in 1572 into a Catholic family, his mother being descended from the sister of Sir Thomas More. They were comfortably well off, although his father, a prosperous merchant, died when Donne was about four years old. Donne proceeded to follow the pattern of life set by his membership in the affluent merchant-class. To be sure, he had to suffer the inconveniences of being a Catholic. The family, however, was not fanatically dedicated to the Counter-Reformation, but rather found its identity in the Catholic humanism of Donne's distinguished ancestor, Sir Thomas More.

John's younger brother, Henry Donne, did not share the detached attitude of his family with regard to Catholicism. In 1593, he died of a fever contracted in prison to which he had been committed for harboring a priest. Donne's mother Elizabeth remained a Catholic all her life.

Donne went to both Oxford and Cambridge but was unable to graduate owing to his Catholic connections. When he was twenty, he studied law at Lincoln's Inn. Soon after, this amiable, well-educated, rather directionless young man, having received his patrimony, traveled widely. In 1596, he found himself on Essex's expedition to Cadiz, and in the Azores during the following year. His education and experience were marking him out for a distinguished career at court. In 1598, he entered the civil service and became a confidential agent to Sir Robert Cecil, under whose auspices he met Sir Thomas Egerton, Keeper of the Seal and member of the Privy Council. Sir Thomas was in need of a secretary, a post for which Donne was admirably suited. He was given the appointment and began his career at the center of power.

It was in 1601 that Donne killed his promise of advancement in the civil service and all hope of preferment at court. He married, suddenly and clandestinely, Ann More, the seventeen-year-old niece and ward of his patron, Sir Thomas Egerton. Nothing could have been more disastrous from the point of view of ambition. Ann's father had Donne flung into prison and attempted, without ultimate success, to have the marriage annulled. Naturally, Donne was dismissed from Egerton's service.

Then followed nearly a decade of comparative poverty and relative obscurity. He had no employment and no prospects. He moved away from the court and settled in Mitcham, now a London suburb, then a small village. His one consolation was the partial cause of his ruin and the object of his love, his wife Ann, who, between 1602 and 1615, bore him twelve children, of whom seven survived. During this period, Donne's complex and fiery spirit began the long reflective process that was to lead him into the priesthood of the Church of England. His hunger for transcendence could be satisfied neither by ambition nor by erotic love. What did he, in his deepest self, really want? He was too hurt and confused to know. He lived in a world of flux and change, and his inner world reflected the outer. Sexual ecstasy had been one way out of his confusion, even if only for a fleeting moment. Lovers were able to burn one another up, suffer the bliss of mutual annihilation and mutual discovery, to catch a taste of union beyond the reach of the universal flux, to be afflicted with the glory of transcendence. But brief and fleeting ecstasy was no longer enough.

The change in Donne, during this period, is deep but subtle. It is not the crass and naive rejection of sex in favor of religion, but rather the transfiguration of sexuality by placing it in a religious context. The love of God in Christ is *more* robust, *not* less than erotic love, the latter being an efficacious symbol of the former. Christ is the Lover who brings with him the gift and wound of transcendence.

> How blest I am in this discovering thee.
> To enter in these bonds is to be free.[4]

Before the debacle of 1601 this was "Brilliant boudoir bawdy;" later it developed into "an article of a strong faith."[5]

In 1605, Donne, already having rejected Roman Catholicism, used his pen in assisting Thomas Morton (who was to become Dean of Gloucester and Bishop of Durham) to construct an Anglican apologetic. The Jesuit cardinal, Robert Bellarmine, was seeking to influence Roman Catholics in England, and he needed answering. The year of the Gunpowder Plot, 1605, was a year not only of political intrigue but also of theological polemics.

Through all this, Donne was beginning to come to life. He was working; he was friendly with the Herberts (particularly Lady Danvers, George Herbert's mother); he was writing the *Holy Sonnets.*[6] He had a patron, Lucy, Countess of Bedford. The ten years of "exile" were being used for an inner transformation. He was discovering for himself the Christian religion and rediscovering that "second religion, friendship."[7] Without his friends, Donne would have been unhinged; thus to Sir Henry Goodyer:

> I write from the fireside in my Parler, and in the noise of three gamesome children; and by the side of her, whom because I have transplanted into a wretched fortune, I must labor to disguise that from her by all such honest devices, as giving her my company and discourse . . . As I have much quenched my senses, and disused my body from pleasure, and so tried how I can indure to be mine own grave, so I try now how I can suffer a prison.[8]

So Donne expressed his melancholy to his friend and out of tenderness kept it hidden from his wife. He was still lost and wounded, but he was on the mend. The hope of resurrection was stirring within him. In Donne's own mind he "died" in 1601 when his fortunes were shattered.[9] This death experience was part of that process of initiation and rebirth which all human beings encounter if they are to grow. By 1608, Donne was looking for a place in the world again, not out of ambition but rather out of the realization that community, social intercourse, the general commerce of society, were necessary if he was to begin to live again. But how was this to be accomplished? What could he do? In September, Donne, very much alive, wrote to Sir Henry Goodyer:

> I would not that death should take me asleep . . . When I must shipwrack, I would do it in a sea where my impotencie might have some excuse; not in a sullen weedy lake, where I could not have so much exercise for my swimming. Therefore I would fain do something; but that I cannot tell what, is no wonder. For to chuse, is to do; but to be no part of anybody, is to be nothing. At most, the greatest persons, are but great wens, and excresences; men of wit and delightfull conversation, but as moales for ornament, except they be so incorporated into the body of the world, that they contribute something to the sustenation of the whole.[10]

Donne wanted to be swimming again. To be human is to be "involved in mankind." To be no part of anybody is to be nothing. The death of a fellow human being involves personal diminishment. But all this he was to write more eloquently in his *Devotions* some fifteen years later. Meanwhile, two more years of the grave and prison of Mitcham had to be endured.

The turning point came in 1610 when Donne wrote a "Funeral Elegie" on the death of Elizabeth Drury, the fourteen-year-old daughter of Sir Robert Drury. The Elegie was so well received that from 1610 to 1612 Donne was given the use of a house in Drury Lane. His fortunes were on the mend. He was on the move again, no less firmly than in the days before 1601, but now with a sense of direction, a sense which had been painfully won. On January 23, 1615, he "received a new character."[11] John King, Bishop of London, ordained John Donne priest.

> For through many straights, and lands I roame,
> I launch at paradise, and I saile towards home.[12]

Soon after his ordination, Donne was appointed chaplain to James I, and in 1616 he was given the post of Reader in Divinity to the students at Lincoln's Inn, which post required him to preach fifty times a year. In 1617, Ann, his wife, died, and another part of Donne died too. In November, 1621, he was made Dean of St. Paul's, and this last decade of his life was continually marred by ill health. In 1623, the year of the *Devotions,* he was seriously ill and during the last summer of 1630, he contracted his final illness. He prepared himself for death, made his will on December 13, and forced himself from his bed to preach what was to be called his own funeral sermon, "Death's Duell," on the first Friday in Lent, 1631. He died on March 31 of that year.

For the purposes of this essay we shall concentrate on the prose works of John Donne. There are 160 sermons extant,[13] and it is to his preaching we shall most frequently turn. It is there that we shall find the true Donne. He gives of himself in the pulpit. Messenger and message are intertwined—a quality that T. S. Eliot found unpalatable. That Donne should use his sermons as a vehicle of self-expression is a mark of inferiority (thought Eliot), hence Eliot's preference for the "purer" but painfully convoluted sermons of Lancelot Andrewes.[14] Whether Eliot is right matters little. Donne, rather than Andrewes, is the man for our time. The visibility of Christ and man's transcendent destiny were the themes upon which Donne improvised and composed his thrilling harmonies and soaring descants. Izaak Walton, Donne's hagiographer, if not biographer, at least knew the Dean of St. Paul's. He had sat at his feet. Walton described Donne as:

> Preaching the Word so, as shewed his own heart was possest with those very thoughts, and joyes that he labored to distill into others: a Preacher in earnest, weeping sometimes for his Auditory, sometimes with them: always preaching to himself, like an Angel from a cloud, but in none . . .[15]

"Always preaching to himself": always struggling to *be* what he preached, a gospel, a word of Good News. How could he avoid using his sermons as a vehicle for self-expression? To preach the Gospel was to preach Christ. To preach Christ was to preach God's word about ourselves. Donne's near ten years of exile had been the proving ground for his vigorous Christology. He was no sentimentalist. He had, in true Augustinian fashion, looked sin and death in the face, he had lusted and loved, he had seen the vanity of this world and caught a glimpse of its promised transfiguration. Like Augustine, he was a doctor of grace, living on borrowed time, a Lazarus who had come back from the dead. Mortality was real, desperately real, but resurrection was a present event. No wonder his sermons burst with energy, with impatience, and with compassion. He was a living icon to his age, of transcendence, a sign that there was more, not only above and beyond man but within him, in the dark richness of what a later poet was to call the "inscape." John Donne is a man for our time, and a sign of that saving transcendence which is focused in Christ, the key to human identity, God's word to me about myself.

Visibility of Christ and the Affliction of Transcendence

Donne was not only a Christian, he was an Anglican. This is an important particular since he incarnates Christianity in its Anglican form. Anglicanism is notoriously difficult to define, and it is of little use looking for definitions in formularies. The spirit of Anglicanism is best discovered in the lives of its most distinguished practitioners. There are those who equal John Donne, there are none who surpass him. He expresses Anglicanism at its best, not the woolly compromise of the *via media*, but the comprehensiveness, the compassion, and the liberality of the *via regia!* Theologically, Anglicanism is incarnational, that is, pragmatic, functional, earthy without losing sight of the fact that this world has a transcendent reference.

Anglicanism as lived by John Donne was not the safe, stodgy thing that some have mistaken for the true marks of English Christianity. To be a vigorous Anglican in the seventeenth century was an exciting and unnerving enterprise. Anglicans then, as now, resisted ready-made answers. These ready-made answers were to be found uncompromisingly in Geneva and Rome. Anglicans were determined to find another way. The Caroline Divines look solid and attractive behind the haze of seventeenth-century prose. We easily forget that an archbishop could lose his head, and a king his, for Anglican principles. Donne lived in the decades which led to the Civil War, to the execution of a king and an archbishop, and to the persecution of the Church. Such was the cradle of Anglicanism.

We have seen something of the life and events which shaped Donne's personality. We now must attempt to enter his mind. Baconian rationalism held no attractions for him, not because he refused to accept the new science, but because he quickly realized that explanations of phenomena actually *explain* nothing. Explanations merely describe phenomena in a new way, albeit in a useful and illuminating one. In its limited fashion the new mode of looking at the world was perfectly acceptable to Donne. What he resisted was the reductionist tendencies of the new age. To exclude mystery, to lose the transcendental dimension, to miss the interconnectedness of things was to leave everything dead and spiritless, to rob everything of significance. Donne's age, like our own, cried out for a "metaphysic," an overview of the world which would harmonize all the discordant elements, would make sense of all the disordered fragments of experience. "Metaphysical," explains Basil Willey:

> meant the capacity to live in divided and distinguished worlds, and to pass freely to and from between one and the other, to be capable of many and varied responses to experience, instead of being confined to a few stereotyped ones . . . The point about these different worlds was not that they were divided, but that they were simultaneously available . . . I think that something of the peculiar quality of the "metaphysical" mind is due to the fact of its not being *finally committed* to any one world. Instead, it could hold them all in a loose synthesis together, yielding itself, as only a mind in free poise can, to the passion of detecting analogies and correspondences between them.[16]

In our chaotic pluralism, we need a new breed of metaphysicals who will be possessed by the passion for analogies and correspondences; men and women with the ability to move freely between and live *simultaneously* in different worlds. Donne could do this. He refused to capitulate to the either/or mentality. He was resolved to be a modern but a believing modern. His was a metaphysic not built up out of speculative philosophy by which men seek to disguise the untidy paradoxes of existence, but one which was formed out of having experienced these "contrareities" in his own personal history. Thus, Donne's paradoxes, his epigrammatic style, his use of puns were not only for the sake of wit but also reflect his vision of reality. He struggled toward a unified vision but:

> Contrariness and ambiguity Donne came to see . . . are in the very fiber of things . . . The elemental fact of ambivalence is that it demands co-existence and complementarity.[17]

The sense of complementarity, the apprehension of the interconnectedness of things, comes at a high price. Donne's scintillating, if undisciplined, intellect could have led him into the indifference of a donnish existence, or into the casual cynicism of politics. His intuition, his "psychic sense of smell" and his second religion, friendship, transformed his cynicism into a healthy skepticism. In the end, he realized that the ambiguities of existence could only be resolved in the painful unitive experience of love. He was excited by his sense of the pervasive unity underlying phenomena. He came to this sense of cohesion not by conceptual thought but by what R.E. Hughes has called "mandalas of experience."[18] Donne reflects on his own experience, and that reflected experience becomes an icon through which he perceives all that there is:

> I was built up scarce fifty years ago in my mother's womb, and I was cast down almost 6,000 years ago in Adam's loins. I was born in the last Age of the world and died in the first.[19]

His own experience serves as a beam of light to illuminate human history and ultimate reality. Donne was never embarrassed by the particular, nor by the basic stuff of things. Earthiness does not cause the sacred to evaporate. It is its prerequisite. Without clods of earth, without the flesh, spirit can never have expression. Knowledge is "a terrestriall Spirit."[20] Donne, the learned Doctor in Divinitie, knew that no less than Donne the lover: the particularity of venereal pleasures in the early years served to reinforce the use of the particular in his decanal sermons.

So there was in Donne an unusually creative unity of intellect and emotion, what T. S. Eliot called:

> A direct sensuous apprehension of thought or a recreation of thought into feeling . . . A thought to Donne was an experience; it modified his sensibility.[21]

This is the heart of Donne's genius: his ability to translate thought into feeling without degenerating into sentimental-

ity. He did this by a painful process of sifting and discrimina-
tion. Hence his thoughts were tested, honed, assayed before
they were transmuted into feeling. He was unafraid intellectually. His work on suicide, "Biathanatos" (which Evelyn Simpson dates around 1609), reveals his "capacity for understanding
and sympathy even in one of the darker areas of Christian
speculation."[22] He was unafraid spiritually as the sermons
testify. To be sure, he was full of Godly fear but was unafraid
of the power of men. He could expose his deepest struggle of
spirit in apparently trivial things:

> I throw my selfe down in my Chamber, and I call in, and invite
> God, and his Angels thither, and when they are there, I neglect
> God and his Angels, for the noise of a Flie, for the ratling of a
> Coach, for the whining of a doore; I talke on, in the same posture
> of praying; Eyes lifted up; knees bowed downe; as though I prayed
> to God; and if God, or his Angels should aske me, when I thought
> last of God in that prayer, I cannot tell; sometimes I finde that I
> had forgot what I was about, but when I began to forget it I cannot
> tell. A memory of yesterdays pleasures, a feare of tomorrows dan-
> gers, a straw under my knee, a noise in mine eare, a light in mine
> eye, an anything, a nothing, a fancy, a Chimera in my braine,
> troubles me in my prayer. So certainely is there nothing, nothing
> in spirituall things, perfect in this world.[23]

I have quoted Donne on the subject of distractions in prayer
at some length for two reasons: to demonstrate his honesty and
to wonder at his depth. This passage is in marked contrast to
the pious clichés concerning prayer which one reads today.
Donne's voice comes through three centuries with authentic
clarity.

What Donne says about prayer can be said about dogma.
There is "nothing in spirituall things, perfect in this world."
There are no perfect creeds, formularies, articles, or confes-
sions. Meaning trapped in language can easily slip away. This
does not mean that nothing meaningful can be said, nothing
significant affirmed. It does mean that reality will not be
trapped. Donne's belief in God was certain, but it was a cer-

tainty springing from sensibility, from Donne's having "a direct sensuous apprehension of thought." He *felt* his thoughts. He did his thinking as he did his praying, with his mind in his heart. He could be as hard on the intellectuals tending towards atheism as he was on the Puritans and Papists veering always towards dogmatism.

> Poore intricated soule! Riddling, perplexed, labyrinthicall soule. Thou couldest not say, that thou beleevest not in God, if there were no God; If there were no God, thou couldest not speake, thou couldest not thinke, not a word, not a thought, no not against God.[24]

God was the prerequisite even for doubting his existence. Donne, the Augustinian, would always insist on the priority of God and the doctrine of prevenient grace. But his hard-won new mode of sensibility would not allow dogma to degenerate into mere explanations of mysteries. This was his main quarrel with the Church of his birth. Seventeenth-century Catholicism wanted to explain everything. Donne hated *quomodo* theology; that is, theology which eviscerated mystery by a too neat explanation, a theology which flattened out all untidy paradoxes. "He that can finde no comfort in this Doctrine . . . till he can expresse *Quo Modo*, robs himself of a great deale of peaceful refreshing."[25] Dominic Baker-Smith writes:

> It was the question of *quomodo* which elicited the fatal answer of transubstantiation, and to Donne the Roman Church, as he understood it, came to be the Church of *quomodo*, translating the Gospel into definitions and formulae that seemed indifferent to human response. In the same spirit he objects to an insensitive theology with sacraments *ex opere operato* as automatic and self-contained means of grace.[26]

Rome was too mechanistic, too regimented for Donne. The intimacy of the divine-human encounter was lost, forfeited in the intricacies of explanation, by seeking to "imprison Christ *in opere operato.*"[27]

Theology, as explanation, stultified the mind. *Roma locuta, causa finita.* Surely there was room for the mind to stretch a little, to doubt, to believe with a deeper sensibility. So Donne preached:

> To come to a doubt, and to a debatement in any religious duty, is the voyce of God in our conscience: Would you know the truth? Doubt, and then you will inquire: And *facile solutionem accipit quo prius dubitavit,* sayes S. Chrysostome.[28]

For Donne we live *within* the Mystery of God. It cannot be objectified. But within that Mystery we can question, probe, examine and come face to face with the mystery which is ourselves. In Dominic Baker-Smith's suggestive phrase, "The individual must expose himself to reality—and this means ultimately to God with an arduous passivity."[29] *An arduous passivity*—there is a phrase which Donne could have understood and embraced. In a later age, Donne would have been called a Barthian, in this respect at least, that before God man is nothing. That man was created to be someone is a sheer act of unmerited grace. Life comes to man as gift not as right. Henri de Lubac states the fundamental paradox which Donne experienced in his flesh: Man

> has that "unstable ontological constitution" which makes it at once something greater and something less than itself. Hence that kind of dislocation, that mysterious lameness, due not merely to sin, but primarily and more fundamentally to be a creature made out of nothing which, astoundingly, touches God ... At once, and inextricably both "nothing" and "image;" fundamentally nothing, yet nonetheless substantially image.[30]

This beautifully expresses the Christian mystery incarnate in John Donne: the unstable ontological constitution, the dislocation, the mysterious lameness, to be at once both nothing and image—this Donne, *viscera et membra,* knew. Thus, constitutionally, he was unable to be a *quomodo* theologian. It was impossible for such a man, for whom paradox was a fire that burned within him, to slip into an easy conceptualizing of reality, to transmute faith into the science of *quomodo.* Lesser minds are tempted to come to an easy solution by coming down on one side of the mystery or the other: man is either nothing or image; he cannot be both. Gregory Palamas expressed his contempt for this either/or mentality in a way which makes one realize how Orthodox Donne was in his apophatic approach to theology:

> the most venerable theologians . . . teach us two things. First they tell us that the divine essence is incommunicable: then, that it is in some way communicable: they tell us that we participate in the nature of God, and that we do not participate in it at all. We must, therefore, hold both assertions, and set them together as the rules of the true faith.[31]

Donne held both together in that mysterious lameness, that affliction of transcendence, which marks our humanity. He managed to come to some sort of equilibrium by using his brilliant intellect in order to dethrone it. He cultivated a compassionate detachment to "see all things despoyl'd of fallacies."[32] This involved hard intellectual discipline. Since intellect and emotion, in Donne, were so contracted that one infused and informed the other, the discipline of the intellect involved the stripping of the self. Stripping the intellect of pedantry and mere cleverness could be done only by a spirit that was recollected in meditation, in prayer, in spiritual discipline. Without that stripping down, the theologian becomes a "spungie slacke Divine,"[33] an intellectual and spiritual parasite, a plagiarist of the soul, living vicariously off the hard-won scholarship and the soul's anguish of others.

"At the centre of the self," writes Dominic Baker-Smith, "is memory—'the Holy Ghost's Pulpit'—containing the collective history that is the Bible and the private history that is the individual."[34] Without recollection, both collective and personal, the soul has no room to grow. The model the Church of Rome offered, so it seemed to Donne, was too mechanistic. It did not do justice to reality as a living organism in which the principles both of continuity and change were at work. Yet, Rome was powerful and articulate. It needed answering.

Donne's attack on Roman Catholicism, "Ignatius and His Conclave" (a satire, genial in tone considering the times), was written in Latin in 1610 and soon translated into English. In the satire the author is transported to hell "in extasie" to witness Igantius argue his way into hell as a troublesome innovator. Ignatius uses his most persuasive arguments to win for himself a place in the infernal regions over the claims of his rival, Machiavelli. Donne "consistently makes fun of his own learning, and of the dreariness of much contemporary philosophy."[35] His attack on Rome uncovers his essential Anglicanism.

Perhaps the *locus classicus* of Donne's Anglicanism is in his sermon preached on the Conversion of St. Paul, 1630.[36] His text was Acts XXIII 6–7:

> But when Paul perceived that one part were Sadducees, and the other Pharisees, he cried out in the Council, Men and Brethren, I am a Pharisee, and the son of a Pharisee; of the hope and resurrection of the dead I am called in question. And when he had said so, there arose a dissention between the Pharisees and the Sadducees and the multitude was divided.

Donne is as politically astute as Paul and might have cried out, "I am a Catholic and the son of a Catholic!" The multitude was divided as Roman Catholics and Protestants have been divided, except in one particular. What united many of the Roman and Genevan persuasions was their common amazement and puzzlement at the Anglican position: the much maligned *via media*. Here is Donne's brilliant exposition:

> Beloved, there are some things in which all Religions agree: The worship of God; The holiness of life; And therefore, if when I study this holinesse of life, and fast and pray, and submit my selfe to discreet, and medicinall mortifications, for the subduing of my body, any man will say, this is Papisticall, Papists doe this, it is a blessed Protestation, and no man is the lesse a Protestant, nor the worse a Protestant for making it. Men and brethren, I am a Papist, that is, I will fast and pray as much as any Papist, and enable my

selfe for the service of my God, as seriously, as laboriously as any Papist. So, if when I startle and am affected at a blasphemous oath, as at a wound upon my Saviour, if when I avoyd the conversation of those men, that prophane the Lords day, any other will say to me, This is Puritanicall, Puritans do this, It is a blessed Protestation, and no man is the lesse a Protestant, nor the worse a Protestant for making it, Men and Brethren, I am a Puritan, that is, I wil endeavour to be pure, as my Father in heaven is pure, as far as any Puritan.[37]

This is a superb example of that elusive thing, Anglican style. It hinges on being able to tolerate a *may* where the dogmatist would demand a *must:*

Their *may*, came to a *must*, those things which were done before *de facto*, came at last to the articles of Faith, and *de jure*, must be beleeved and practised upon salvation. They chide us for going away, and they drove us away.[38]

It would help to focus Donne's "cosmic" Anglicanism by examining his doctrine of the Church, whose sole object is to "contemplate Christ clearly and uniformly."[39] The dissension, the internecine war, the polemics of Rome, of Geneva and Canterbury all distressed him because they marred the face of Christ in the world. He knew too much of the theological warfare within the Roman Church to be persuaded that the sure ark of salvation was the Bark of Peter. Rome could not come through with what she promised. Her claims regarding this life properly belonged to the life to come.

Donne believed that the task of the Church was to make Christ visible to the world. If Rome wanted to impress Anglicans with her extravagant claims, she should first set her own house in order.

Let me see a Dominican and a Jesuit reconciled, in doctrinall papistry, for free will and predestination. Let me see a French papist and an Italian papist reconciled in state-papistry, for the Pope's jurisdiction. Let me see the Jesuits and the secular priests reconciled in England, and when they are reconciled to one another, let them presse reconciliation to their Church.[40]

We must remember that Donne was writing in the early seventeenth century: the century of Catholic killing Protestant, of Protestant Catholic, of Anglican Puritan, and Puritan Anglican. It was tragic that Donne's countrymen were unable to receive his word. Perhaps we can hear it now over three centuries later. It surely has an uncanny contemporary ring and speaks to the present need of the Church to proclaim the uniqueness of Christ without lapsing into ecclesiastical megalomania. Donne's vision, even today, seems startlingly contemporary, perhaps ahead of us, too. Donne felt in his bones the movement toward integration through the painful "contrarieties" of experience. True, he had no experience of the Jungian-Freudian Exodus which has enabled us to enter simultaneously the Promised Land and the Wasteland. Yet he anticipated our experience of reality, and our understanding of the Church as that of the Exodus, as a nomadic, pilgrim reality. Life was a peregrination and the Church, for Donne, was the Caravan. Mankind thus recapitulates the Exodus. The Church is on the march from Egypt to Jerusalem.

First, this Exodus has to be subjective and personal, and only then can we proceed to the objective and communal. There is no value in proclaiming a universal Gospel unless that Gospel be for *me*. There is no point in promulgating a doctrine of the Church as the body of Christ, unless I have been engrafted into Christ who is its Head. Thus Donne writes:

> As thou hast enlightened and enlarged me to contemplate thy greatness, O God, descend thou and stoop down to see my infirmities and the Egypt in which I live; and (If thy good pleasure be such) hasten mine *Exodus* and deliverance, for I desire to be dissolved, and be with thee.[41]

Provisions for our Exodus are to be found in the Scriptures and in the Sacraments, and these are the twin pillars on which the Church is founded. The Bible, as interpreted by the Church, gives the direction. It is the compass. The Sacraments, as administered by the Church, provide sustenance for the journey. In the Church, individual and collective considerations are beautifully poised, and only in the Church is their true balance. In interpreting Scripture and administering the Sacraments:

> The Church is providing the occasion, the composition of place as it were, for contact with God, but the final step, the colloquy, remains the responsibility of the individual. . . . What emerges is an extremely delicate relationship between the Church and the believer designed to allow a maximum of personal responsibility within the framework of Catholic tradition . . . the *via media*, so often dismissed as genial compromise, can demand the kind of alert discrimination that emerges from Donne's habit of mind. His awareness of himself as primarily a Christian rather than a member of a specific Church is itself an Anglican characteristic.[42]

Donne was a moderate Erasmian Catholic, the *via media* being the *via regia* between Protestants and papistici.[43] The important thing to remember is that the Church is *in via*, "the Church is in a warfare, the Church is in a pilgrimage and therefore there is not setling."[44]

There is, argues Donne, no evidence for the existence of a Church which "must bee *Super-Catholicke*, and *Super-Universall* above all the *Churches* of the world."[45] *Ubi libellus?* "Where is your evidence?" There is no evidence unless we mistake the superedifications for foundations: "The peace of the Church, the plenty of the Church, the ceremonies of the Church, the *sua*, but not *illa*, they are hers but they are not she."[46]

All the powers of Donne's intellect were required to maintain the equilibrium between the personal and the collective in his understanding of the Church. The Church is founded upon that Rock which is Christ, but it is not itself the Rock capable of claiming infallible "locall and personall succession."[47] Any claim to succession in human terms must face the fact of historical interruption. The catholicity of the Church is a gift and a peculiarly eschatological one. It is slippery and elusive, and because of this one is tempted to locate this catholicity in the *sua;* in its ceremonies and polity, and not in the *illa* which is Christ and "his inestimable benefits." Repentance, the forgiveness of sins, the death and resurrection of Christ "are that *Doctrine* which coagulates and gathers the Church into a body and makes it Catholicke."[48]

Anglicanism, Catholic and Reformed, prides itself on its "mediocrity," in the sense in which Donne used the word.[49] It is the way of moderation without lukewarmness. It means being poised in a middle state between two extremes. It can be said that the Anglican Church, at its best, is mediocre, in the seventeenth-century meaning of the word. At its worst, it is mediocre in the twentieth-century sense. The word enthusiasm also comes to mind in both its ancient and modern senses: "the severe and unrectified Zeal" of the one and the bracing challenge of the other. The Church of England sought to be unenthusiastic in the former sense, at the risk of falling into being unenthusiastic in the latter. Anglicanism is moderate in insisting on the contingent nature of most things ecclesiastical, and in refusing to think of them as necessary. That this can be weakness must be admitted. Essentials sometimes get lost in the Anglican passion for moderation. It is a matter of indifference to the Anglican, John Donne, that there are several Churches with different polities and customs since there is, in essence, "but one Church, journying to one Hierusalem, and directed by one guide, Christ:

> Jesus . . . In my poor opinion the form of Gods worship, established in the Church of *England* be more convenient and advantageous than of any other Kingdome, both to provide and kindle devotion, and also fix it, that it stray not into infinite expansion and Subdivisions; (into the former of which, Churches utterly despoyl'd of Ceremonies seem to me to have fallen; and the *Roman* Church, by presenting innumerable objects, into the latter).[50]

Just so Anglicanism, to its adherents, seems to be "more convenient." That is all. That is sufficient. This does not mean one is not an Anglican by conviction, but rather that Anglicanism can never be an object of faith.

Visibility of Christ and the Affliction of Transcendence

The catholicity of the Church is a *given* which unifies all the contradictions, paradoxes, tensions and polarities of existence. The Church gives Donne's passionate individualism an anchor, a place in which to breathe freely and move about openly. It is not the charnel-house of the soul, it is the ground of its existence.

Perhaps Donne's most famous passage concerning the catholicity of the Church is to be found in his "Devotions upon Emergent Occasions," written during a period of severe illness and published in 1624. The doctrine of the Church emerges from Donne's reflection on his experience. Thought is transmuted into feeling:

> The *Church* is *Catholicke, universal,* so are all her *Actions; All* that she does, belongs to *all.* When she *baptizes a child,* that action concerns mee; for that this child is thereby converted to that *Head* which is my *Head* too, and engrafted in that body, whereof I am a *member.*[51]

Donne's sense of his solidarity with the human race does not, in the end, contradict his sense of uniqueness. Mankind has a common end: death which unites us all in a common hope. Mankind is all of a piece, and we are united by the tolling of a bell. *Nunc lento sonitu dicunt, Morieris.*[52] Such is our common catholic end.

It is this basic fact which informs Donne's attitude to others and gives impetus to his preaching and fire to his sense of mission. It was Donne who preached the first Anglican Missionary sermon to the Honourable Company of the Virginian Plantation on November 13, 1622.[53] The first white English child had been baptized only thirty-five years earlier by the Reverend Thomas Hariot. Her name was Virginia Dare—a suitable name for the occasion!

The alliance between evangelical zeal and commercial venture was, as one would expect, short-lived. Donne had a doubly difficult task in preaching to the merchant adventurers in 1622.[54] Not only had he to outline, for the members of the Company, their Christian duty toward the original inhabi-

tants of Virginia, the Indians, but he had to do this in the face
of recent news that these very Indians had killed around 350
English settlers that same year. The fact that Donne's words
fell on deaf ears is tragic, since 1622 begins the process of the
elimination of the Indian in North America. Nevertheless, the
fact that he preached as he did is remarkable. Earlier that year,
on Easter Monday, Donne had proclaimed:

> A Man is thy Neighbour, by his Humanity not by his Divinity; by
> his Nature, not by his Religion: A Virginian is thy neighbor, as
> well as a Londoner; and all men are in every good man's Diocese,
> and Parish.[55]

This was Donne's method. Begin with what is given, that is
what is natural and build on that. The doctrine of the Church
is grounded in our common humanity, a fact that the Virgini-
ans soon forgot and which most men choose to repress. Donne
does not despise commercial enterprise, man's natural desire
for position and place. He builds on this brilliantly. He is
careful for the prerogatives of King Charles, but more careful
for those of the King of Kings. He presents to the Honourable
Company of the Virginian Plantation an image of the Pilgrim
Church which needs revival today:

> You shall have made this *Iland,* which is but as the *Suburbs* of the
> old world, a Bridge, a Gallery to the new; to joyne all to that world
> that shall never grow old, the Kingdome of heaven, You shall add
> persons to this Kingdome and to the Kingdome of heaven, and add
> names to the Bookes of our Chronicles, and to the Booke of Life.[56]

Donne, the metaphysical, could live simultaneously in two
worlds: in the world of England in 1622 and the world in which
human brotherhood and solidarity was already an accomplished fact. He saw that eschatological dimension of the
Church which always anticipates the end. He lived within that
vision and it made and marred him as a man and as a Christian.
He poured himself out in the attempt to articulate this vision,
to make visible the Christ, to share with others the glorious

affliction of transcendence, the affliction that man is driven always to be *more*.

The Church itself was the sacrament of this transcendence, it was the arena in which Christ was made present and visible. It was a meeting place for all the warring elements in Donne's soul, a place of wholeness, of totality, of participation. R.E. Hughes writes:

> For the central fact of Donne is that he is a man who expended himself entirely and who in grasping the particularities of experience found himself clutching at a universal.[57]

Christ, for Donne, was the dazzling particular which focused the universal, not in any easy or naive way since he was well "aware of the tough edges of existence *within* which divinity was manifest."[58] Transcendence was not "up there," or "outside" but within the fabric of the world, within the labyrinth of the soul. Christ was the reality which both infused his flesh and held the world in being.

Donne knew this from bitter experience and crushing disappointment. As a young man, he had misunderstood the glorious reality of divinized flesh. The Word became Flesh was turned upside down so that the Flesh became the Word: an easy but fatal error. Nevertheless, the fleshliness of his poetry is that which, in the end, gives sacramental depth to his theology. Nothing is wasted. He knew that love, to *be* love, has to be particular, has to be enfleshed. He knew also that love involves the surrendering of the self. He knew that extinction is a prerequisite for resurrection. His creative preoccupation with death is the leit-motif of his thrilling resurrection sermons. In Christ he perceives that sexuality, marvelous as it is, is but the potent symbol of an even more robust love.

Christ, like all human beings, is unfathomable. He cannot be totally understood. He can, however, be touched and embraced. Every human being is a mystery which is simultaneously palpable and unfathomable. We live the paradox. Every human heart, like the Divine Essence, is both communicable and incommunicable, *at the same time*.

Christ is both alchemist and elixir. He makes the cure and he is the cure. He is the *aurum potabile* which transforms our wounded nature, and enables us to live the mystery and begin to see at least some resolution to the apparent contradictions of existence. He it is who transfigures our either/or into both/and.

> He was all gold when he lay downe, but rose
> All tincture, and doth not alone dispose
> Leaden and iron will to good, but is
> Of power to make even sinfull flesh like his.[59]

This was the miracle of the incarnation: the visibility of the Invisible God, in which we are invited to participate. Ours is a journey to the divinizing of our flesh, a movement from darkness to light. The compass for this hazardous adventure is:

> the essential Word of God, the Son of God, *Christ Jesus* . . . He was God, *humbled in the flesh*; he was Man *received into glory* . . . Here is the compass of all time, as time was distributed in the Creation, *Vespere* & *mane*; darkness, and then light: the Evening and the Morning made the day .[60]

God not only provides the Compass for our journey but also our sustenance along the way: *"the visible sacraments, "*[61] made of palpable and digestible elements, bread and wine and water. It is thus that divinity is manifested in the fabric of the world, that world which Donne never understated nor undervalued. It takes time to learn to perceive divinity. It is a hard school in which particulars are sifted, sorted and rejected until *the* Particular emerges which is the icon of the universal. The Christian is the one who has graduated from the grammar school of typology, that is the fascination with minutiae, with instances, and entered the university of the Logos, "from *exempla* to the living presence of Christ."[62] Christ is present in and to the stuff of things, if only we could see.

Visibility of Christ and the Affliction of Transcendence

It is the task of the preacher to proclaim the visibility of Christ, the Word, to help man see that the affliction of transcendence is the wound-mark of divinity.

> Christ is *verbum*, the Word; not a word, but The Word: The Minister is *vox*, voice; not a voice, The voice, the voice of that word and no other . . . and speaking according to his dictate; and pleasing to them to whom he is sent by bringing the Gospel of Peace and Reparation to all wounded and scattered and contrite Spirits.[63]

This is a heavy burden for the preacher and gives us some idea of how Donne viewed the priesthood. To preach the Word one had to live it, breathe it, be in love with it. Once one has encountered the living Word which is Christ, everything changes. St. Paul was the great example of a transfigured life, a man transformed by the "real presence of Christ," by the visibility of God.

> Here was a true Transubstantiation, and a new Sacrament. These few words, *Saul, Saul, why persecutest thou me,* are words of a consecration; after these words, *Saul* was no longer *Saul,* but he was Christ: *Vivit in me Christus,* says he.[64]

Man himself was to be the living sacrament of Christ's visibility in the world. To do this man has to be converted. He has to be consecrated, to be transubstantiated, by a descent into nothingness because "there is a good nullification of heart, a good bringing of the heart to nothing."[65] This nullification, this mortification is the prelude to a new creation.

> When . . . I come to such a melting and pouring out of my heart, that there be no spirit, that is, none of mine own spirit left in me; when I have so exhausted, so evacuated myself, that is all confidence in myself, that I come into the hands of my God, as pliably, as ductily, as that first clod of earth, of which he made me in *Adam* . . . this is a blessed nullification of the heart. When I say to my self . . . *I am nothing;* and then say to God, Lord, though I be nothing, yet behold, I present thee as much as thou hadst to make the whole world of; O thou that mad'st the whole world of nothing, make me, that am nothing in my own eyes, a new Creature in Christ Jesus: This is a blessed nullification, a glorious annihilation of the heart.

So is there also a blessed nullification thereof, in the contrition of heart, in the sense of my sins; when, as a sharp winde may have work out a Marble Statue . . . so my holy tears, made holy in his Blood that gives them a tincture . . . have worn out my Marble Heart, . . . and emptied the room of that former heart, and so give God a *Vacuity*, a new place to create a heart in.[66]

This is the creative emptiness of the mystic who understands his very being to be essentially *capax Dei* and therefore in need of emptying in order to be filled. The more we are full of ourselves, the less life there is in us. Christ came precisely to take our "nothing" and make it "someone." It is this nothing that we truly are which we must offer to God in order that he may create us anew, *ex nihilo*. God was in Christ to save us from the ultimate absurdity, this emptiness which is despair, the vacuity which is spiritual exhaustion. The salvation offered in Christ is both free and universal: two facts unpalatable to those who would count God's elect or limit his salvation.

To save this body from the condemnation of everlasting corruption, where the wormes that we breed are our betters, because they have life, where the dust of dead kings is blowne into the street, and the dust of the street is blowne into the River, and the muddy River tumbled into the Sea, and the Sea remaunded into all the veynes and channels of the earth; to save this body from everlasting dissolution, dispersion, dissipation, and to make it in a glorious Resurrection, not onely a Temple of the holy Ghost, but a Companion of the holy Ghost in the kingdome of heaven, This *Christ* became this *Jesus.*[67]

(It must have been magnificent to hear these words straight from the preacher's mouth.) Thus Donne proclaims the Incarnation. To reject this free gift either by excluding others or excluding the self is the deepest folly. One action smacks of tyranny and usurpation, the other as rebellious melancholy.

No one could accuse Donne of not having an adequate and deep sense of sin in general, and of his own sin in particular. The question is, which is the greater, man's sin or God's love? To exalt the former at the expense of the latter is disproportionate and a subtle form of pride, even in this inordinate dejection thou exaltest thy selfe above God, and makest thy worst better than his best, thy sins larger than his mercy. Christ hath a Greek name, and an Hebrew name; *Christ* is Greek, *Jesus* is Hebrew; he had commission to save all nations, and he hath saved all; Thou givest him another name . . . *Abaddon*, and *Apollyn*, a Destroyer; when thou wilt not apprehend him as a Saviour, and love him so.[68]

To deny others the grace of God is to block out Christ, to diminish his visibility, to impoverish God. Sin is the masking of the visibility of Christ to the world by his followers. We have, by our darkening sin, "wounded him, and lam'd him . . . by our oppression, we had need provide God an Hospitall."[69]

The relationship between Christ and the believer is very subtle. Nowhere does Donne suggest that God somehow needs our response in his maintaining the universe. Nor does he suggest that our submission is total annihilation. We are not absorbed into the Godhead but invited to communion. We grieve God, but we do not hamper him. What amazes Donne is the deference and reticence of God. That God would so pour himself out for us is too wonderful. Thus Donne reflects on the divine *kenosis:*

Remember that our Saviour Christ himselfe, in many actions and passions of our humane nature, and infirmities, smothered that Divinity, and suffered it not to worke, but yet it was alwayes in him, and wrought most powerfully in the deepest danger; when he was absolutely dead, it raised him again . . . Christ slumbred the Godhead in himselfe.[70]

God smothers his divinity in Christ for our sake, he lets it slumber in flesh, in the ordinary and the commonplace, in ordinances and sacraments, in bread and wine. We eat and we become what we eat since:

the end of all bodily eating is Assimilation . . . that meat may be made *idem corpus*, the same body that I am; so the end of all spirituall eating is Assimilation too, That after all Hearing, and all Receiving, I may be made *idem spiritus cum Domino.*[71]

Our bodies are the organ in which God breathes. We are
body, mind and Holy Spirit and are human insofar as we have
yielded up that total *vacuity* in which the spirit dwells. The
body, as the Temple of the Holy Ghost, is made in "consulta-
tion of the whole Trinity."[72] The wonder is that God who is
spirit should have such an affection for this earthly body of
ours, and in order to do so allows his divinity to sleep. The
visibility of Christ is not thrust upon us. It is a veiled visibility
for the sake of love. Love is not love when there is force.

> Christ saves no man against his will. There is a word crept into the
> later school, that deludes many a man; they call it *Irrestibility*
> . . . Christ beats his Drum, but he does not Press men; Christ is
> serv'd with Voluntaries.[73]

The life of Christ was a continual *kenosis*. In the light of the
seventeenth-century mood, of its religious intolerance, of the
forces of both Reformation and Counter-Reformation harden-
ing behind the walls of Geneva and Rome, Donne's theology
is all the more remarkable. He preached an open Christ present in all Churches, and while he was not afraid to defend his
Anglicanism, he knew that it was but the form, the fragile
shell of a universal Gospel. Men may rage and rant. Christ, the
image of the invisible God, quietly and gently accomplishes
his purpose.

Donne, preaching at St. Paul's on Christmas Day, 1626, continues the *kenosis* theme:

> The whole life of Christ was a continuall Passion; others die Mar-
> tyrs, but Christ was born a Martyr. He found a *Golgotha*, (where
> he was crucified) even in Bethlehem, where he was born; For, to
> his tendernesse then, the strawes were almost as sharp as the
> thornes after; and the Manger as uneasie at first, as his Crosse at
> last. His birth and death were but one continuall act, and his
> Christmas-day and his Good-Friday, are but the evening and
> morning of one and the same day.[74]

There is no place better to catch the visibility of Christ in this
world than in the passion of the poor. There the reticence and
deference are most manifest since the poor is:

Visibility of Christ and the Affliction of Transcendence

Nuda Imago . . . it is much a harder thing, and there is much more art showed in making a *naked picture*, than in all the rich attire that can be put upon it. And howsoever the rich man, that is invested in Power, and Greatnesse, may be a better picture of God, of God considered in himself, who is all Greatnes, all Power, yet of God considered in Christ . . . the poor man is the better picture . . . Christ himself carries this consideration . . . not to a *proximity* onely but to an *identity*, The poore are He . . . He is the poore. And so, he that oppresseth the poore, reproaches God, God in his *Orphans*, God in his *Image*, God in the *Members* of his owne Body, God in the *Heirs* of his Kingdom, God in *himself*, in his own person.[75]

God, in the world and especially in the poor, has a high visibility. He can be seen, touched, handled, abused and betrayed in Christ. There is nothing made which does not manifest him—a gnat, a worm tell me simply, "God is," because "The whole frame of the world is the Theatre, and every creature the stage, the *medium*, the glasse in which we may see God."[76] To be a true atheist a man would have to pluck out his eyes. Look at a blade of grass, a leaf, a lump of rock and sense the presence of the Maker. Nature reveals the *presence* of God but not "the Essence; the secret purposes of God."[77] Revelation is needed for man to interpret what he sees, and Christ is the image of the invisible God.

Donne passed onto others his watchful eye and became for them an icon of the resurrection. Isaak Walton found, in Donne, a lively image of Christ, a mortal frame which was destined not only to become "a small quantity of Christian dust,"[78] but also to be raised to newness of life.

Salvation, for Donne, was nothing less than the recovery of the Trinitarian life in true Augustinian fashion; the recovery of memory, understanding and will. All three he abandoned to God. What is impressive is that for Donne each yielding, each giving up is not a rejection but a transfiguration. Sexuality is not repressed but transcended. Ambition is not denied but its energies redirected. Reason is never incarcerated but truly liberated by knowledge of its limitations. All are perceived as gift, as grace, as gospel. Donne's transfiguration was long, painful and glorious. Its incubation period was the nine years of testing (1601–1610), its fruition in this life, his magnificent funeral sermon "Death's Duell"[79] on that first Friday in Lent, 1631. Donne was ready for death. He knew that:

> Many graines make up the bread that feeds us; and many thornes make up the Crowne that must glorifie us . . . But . . . since that Crown is made of thorns, be not without them when you contemplate Christ . . . Find thorns within; a wounding sense of sin, bring you the thorns, and Christ will make it a crown.[80]

Donne's crown of thorns finally began to form in the fall of 1630, the occasion of his last illness. He was so ill that he could not preach the "Gunpowder Plot Sermon" on November 5th. A dying man eventually climbed into the pulpit of St. Paul's at the beginning of Lent, 1631. In the presence of the King, the dean, marked for death, preached on the death of God, not in terms of the shallow theology of this century, but with the vibrant sensibility of the seventeenth:

> That *God . . . the Lord of life could dye,* is a strange contemplation; That the *red Sea* could bee drie . . . is strange . . . but *supermiraculous* that *God could dye;* but that *God would dye* is an *exaltation* of that. . . . There was nothing more free, more voluntary, more spontaneous than the death of *Christ* . . . There wee leave you in that *blessed dependency,* to *hang* upon him that *hangs* upon the *Crosse,* there *bathe* in his *teares,* there suck at his *wounds,* and *lye downe in peace* in his *grave,* till hee vouchsafe you a *resurrection,* and an ascension into that *Kingdome,* which hee hath *purchas'd* for you, with the *inestimable price* of his *incorruptible blood.* AMEN.[81]

Izaak Walton writes that Donne preached this sermon "as if having done this, there remained nothing for him to doe, but to die."[82] The visibility of Christ in a man prepared to die, the final affliction where the longing for transcendence becomes a reality in the life to come: all this was present in the dying of John Donne. "To be alive, to be able to see, and to know where we are going—is there anything else which matters?"[83] Donne was nowhere more alive than at his departing, his vision never more clear, his destiny never more manifest.

Visibility of Christ and the Affliction of Transcendence

Through a long pilgrimage he had come to know Christ as God's Word about himself.

John Donne and Edward West share in the same calling, in the same priesthood. Both see it as a high calling.

> What a Coronation is our taking of Orders, by which God makes us a Royall Priesthood? . . . That I should not onely be able to say, as Christ said to that poore soule, *Confide fili*, My son be of good comfort, but *Fratres & Patres mei*, My Brethren, and my Fathers, nay *Domini mei*, and *Rex meus*, My Lords, and My King be of good comfort, your sins are forgiven you; That God should seale to me that Patent, *ite praedicite omni Creaturae* . . . That if I finde a licentious Goat, a supplanting Fox, an usurious Wolfe, an ambitious Lion, yet to that creature, to every creature I should preach the Gospel of peace and consolation, and offer these creatures a Metamorphosis, a transformation, a new Creation in Christ Jesus, and thereby make my Goat, my Fox, and my Wolfe, and my Lion, to become *Semen Dei* . . . and *Fillium Dei* . . . and *Participem Divinae Naturae* . . . ; This is which Christ is essentially in himselfe, This is that which ministerially he hath committed to me, to shed his consolation upon you, upon you all.[84]

Edward Nason West, having a measure of Donne's spirit, is a man for our time, because for him all times and all places meet in the creative logos which is Christ. Edward West, too, stands for the visibility of Christ and knows in his own self the wound of transcendence, which comes to those who wrestle with God. "He watches for him whose name is Light."

NOTES

1. Inscription on a marble statue of John Donne by Nicholas Stone. It is in St. Paul's Cathedral, London, and survived the Great Fire of 1666.

2. Robert S. Jackson, *John Donne's Christian Vocation* (Evanston, Ill.: Northwestern University Press, 1970), p. 28.

3. E. N. West, *God's Image in Us* (New York: World Publishing Co., 1960), p. 181.

4. R. E. Hughes, *The Progress of the Soul: The Interior Career of John Donne* (New York: William Morrow, 1968), p. 36.

5. *Ibid.*, p. 37.

6. See his letter to Mrs. Magdalen Herbert, July 1607: *John Donne: Selected Prose*, chosen by Evelyn Simpson and edited by Helen Gardner and Timothy Healy (Oxford: Oxford University Press, 1967), p. 124.

7. See his letter to Sir Henry Goodyer, 1608: *Selected Prose*, p. 125.

8. *Ibid.*, p. 127.

9. Hughes, *Progress*, p. 204: "If at last I must confess, that I died ten years ago . . . yet it will please me a little to have had so long a funeral, and to have kept my self so long above ground without putrefaction." Written from France, 1612.

10. *Selected Prose*, p. 129.

11. *Ibid.*, p. 146. Letter to Sir Edward Herbert, Jan. 25, 1615.

12. John Donne, *The Progresse of the Soule II:* pp. 56–57 (1601), quoted in Hughes, *Progress*, p. 70.

13. *The Sermons of John Donne*, edited by G. R. Potter and Evelyn M. Simpson, 10 vols. (Berkley, California: University of California Press, 1953–1962). Henceforth referred to as *Sermons*.

14. T. S. Eliot, "Lancelot Andrewes," *Selected Essays* (New York: Harcourt Brace & Co., 1932), p. 299ff, quoted in *Essays in Celebration*, edited by A. J. Smith (London: Metheun, 1972), p. 27.

15. *The Sermons of John Donne*, selected by Theo. Gill (New York: Meridien Books, Inc., 1958), p. 5.

16. Basil Willey, *The Seventeenth Century Background* (New York: Doubleday Anchor Books, 1943), p. 50.

17. R.E. Hughes, *Progress*, p. 66.

18. *Ibid.*, p. 198.

19. *Sermons*, VII, p. 78.

20. *Ibid.*, p. 260.

21. Eliot, *Selected Essays*, quoted in *Essays in Celebration*, p. 27.

22. *Selected Prose*, p. 27.

23. *Sermons*, VII, p. 78.

24. *Ibid.*, VIII, pp. 332–33. Sermon preached at St. Paul's in the evening, upon the day of St. Paul's conversion, 1629.

25. *Ibid.*, VII, p. 227.

26. Dominic Baker-Smith, "John Donne's Critique of True Religion," *Essays in Celebration*, p. 413.

27. *Sermons*, VII, p. 267.

28. *Ibid.*, V, p. 38.

29. Baker-Smith, "Donne's Critique," pp. 413–14.

30. Henri de Lubac, *The Mystery of the Supernatural* (London: Geoffrey Chapman, 1967), pp. 147–48.

31. *Ibid.*, p. 218.

32. "The Second Anniversary," *Sermons*, I, p. 295.

33. *Ibid.*, I, p. 328.

34. Baker-Smith, "Donne's Critique," p. 417.

35. *Selected Prose*, p. 59.

36. *Sermons*, IX, p. 162.

37. *Ibid.*, IX, p. 166.

38. *Ibid.*, pp. 170–72. From a Sermon preached at White-Hall.

39. "Essays in Divinity," *Selected Prose*, p. 78.
40. *Sermons*, IV, p. 301. From a Sermon preached at St. Paul's upon Christmas Day, 1622.
41. Evelyn M. Simpson, ed., *Essayes in Divinity* (Oxford: Oxford University Press, 1952), p. 96.
42. Baker-Smith, "Donne's Critique," p. 418.
43. *Ibid.*, p. 421.
44. *Sermons*, IX, p. 332.
45. *Ibid.*, VIII, p. 64.
46. *Ibid.*, IX, p. 332. See also "Essays in Divinity" in *Selected Prose*, pp. 75ff. It is a calamity that the Catholic Church "should in her latter age suffer many convulsions, distractions, rents, schisms, and wounds, by the severe and un-rectified Zeal of many, who should impose necessity upon indifferent things, and oblige all the World to one precise forme of exterior worship, and Ec-clesiastick policie; averring that every degree, and minute and scruple of all circumstances which may be admitted in either beleef or practice, is certainly, constantly, expressly, and obligatorily exhibited in the Scriptures."
47. "Pseudo-Martyr," *Selected Prose*, p. 51.
48. *Ibid.*, p. 43.
49. See *Sermons*, VIII, p. 90, where he praised Lady Danvers' "mediocrity."
50. "Essays in Divinity," *Selected Prose*, p. 77.
51. "Devotions upon Emergent Occasions," *Selected Prose*, pp. 100–101.
52. *Ibid.*
53. *Sermons*, IV, p. 270.
54. Virginia did not become a Royal Province until 1624.
55. *Sermons*, IV, p. 110.
56. *Ibid.*, pp. 280–81.
57. Hughes, *Progress*, pp. 9–10.
58. *Ibid.*
59. *Ibid.*, quoted p. 170.
60. *Sermons*, III, pp. 302–303. (February 16, 1620).
61. *Ibid.*, II, p. 242. Italics mine. See also *Sermons*, VI, p. 69: "God hath not removed man, not withdrawn man from this Earth . . . not only to tread upon it, as in contempt, or in dominion, but to walk upon it, in the discharge of the duties of his calling; and so be conversant with the Earth, is not a falling."
62. *Sermons*, IX, pp. 383–84.
63. *Ibid.*, II, p. 172.
64. *Ibid.*, VI, p. 209.
65. *Ibid.*, IX, p. 177.
66. *Ibid.*
67. *Ibid.*, III, pp. 302–303.
68. *Ibid.*
69. *Ibid.*, IX, p. 301.
70. *Ibid.*, VI, p. 174. John Donne preached this on Christmas Day, 1624.
71. *Ibid.*, p. 223.
72. *Ibid.*, pp. 265–67.
73. *Ibid.*, VII, p. 156.
74. *Ibid.*, p. 279.
75. *Ibid.*, VIII, p. 285.
76. *Ibid.*, p. 224.
77. *Ibid.*, IX, p. 134.

78. Izaak Walton, "The Life of Dr. John Donne" (n.p.: 1640), quoted in R. E. Hughes, *Progress*, p. 7.

79. *Sermons*, X, p. 229f.

80. In a Letter to Sir Thomas Roe, December 1, 1622 quoted by W. Moelwyn Merchant "Donne's Sermon to the Virginia Company, 13 November 1622," in *Essays in Celebration*, p. 438.

81. *Sermons*, X, pp. 229–48.

82. Izaak Walton, "The Life of Dr. John Donne" (n.p.: 1640), quoted in *Selected Prose*, p. 374.

83. West, *God's Image*, p. 181. See note #3.

84. *Sermons*, VII, p. 134.

7

The Reconciliation of Opposites: A Study of St. Francis and von Hügel

A. M. Allchin

IT IS VERY EVIDENT that in the twentieth century, the figure of St. Francis has attracted Christians of every tradition. Men have seen in him not only something of the original purity of the gospel, but also something of its original freedom and inclusiveness. In this article we intend to explore the meaning of this attraction, in relation both to certain theologians of the twentieth century and to the tradition of Eastern Orthodoxy in the centuries before St. Francis and in the period which follows him. In particular we mean to consider the relatedness of one of the greatest Roman Catholic thinkers of our time, Baron Friedrich von Hügel, to the little poor man of Assisi.

Among the counsels which the Abbé Huvelin gave to the Baron, when he visited him in Paris in 1886, is a remark which is liable to strike anyone who is interested in St. Francis. "Yes," said the Abbé, "there have been saints, even great saints, of your type. St. Francis of Assisi . . . *there* is a great saint wholly cast in the mould of life and movement, light and warmth."[1] At first sight, the comparison would seem paradoxical in the extreme. What can there be in common between the two men? On the one side there was the massive, complex, aristocratic intellectual, half English, half German, whose thought, suspected of modernism in his own day, is becoming increasingly influential among theologians at the present time; on the other side there was the little poor man of Assisi, with his passionate, intuitive vision of things and his deep distrust of scholars and their habit of amassing books. Yet the judgment of a man like Huvelin is not to be lightly dismissed. His ministry in Paris was restricted by recurrent ill health, but his influence as a spiritual guide was incalculable, not only in the life of von Hügel, but also in that of Charles de Foucauld, and it is difficult to think of the twentieth-century Church without him. What is more his methods of direction caught the attention of C. G. Jung, who is reported to have found in the work of Huvelin and certain of his contemporaries, an anticipation of his own approach to psychotherapy.

In the case of von Hügel, his influence was profound. Through him it passed into the Church of England, not least through the writings of Evelyn Underhill, whose books, scholarly and popular, did much to make the Baron's position known to readers who would have been daunted by the complexity of his own approach. For Evelyn Underhill stood in relation to von Hügel as von Hügel stood to Huvelin, and transmitted the same message and the same spirit. She drew attention to this comparison of the two so apparently dissimilar figures of the Baron and the poor man in one of her essays on St. Francis. "It is the opinion, she wrote, of a saint, of a realist, for whom God was everything—about two other saints, also realists for whom God was everything; and neither of whom was able to exclude any aspect of his creation from the sphere of their interest and their love. Plainly it is not an opinion based on surface characters, but on some interior likeness which entirely escapes the casual glance."[2]

Before we come to examine this interior likeness between

the two men more closely, it might be well to notice that in our century St. Francis has exercised a fascination for Christians of all kinds, among them a number of distinguished theologians. In the Church of England, Charles Raven would be an outstanding example; a man who, like von Hügel, combined an intense interest in theology with an equal concern for the natural sciences, a man in his own day also suspect as a modernist but now beginning to be more justly valued. But the attraction of St. Francis is not felt only by Anglicans and Protestants. Two of the most eminent theologians of the Russian diaspora, Vladimir Lossky and Paul Evdokimov, were strongly drawn to St. Francis, despite certain evidently Western traits in his character. There is something here which demands further investigation and reflection.

Evelyn Underhill, in the essay from which we have already quoted, is clear enough where the affinity between von Hügel and St. Francis is to be found. It lies in the fact that both men, in their utterly different ways, seek to do justice to the reality both of this world and of the world beyond this one. Their complete dedication to the service of God does not exclude a clear-sighted view of the world which lies around them. "Both the medieval friar and the modern scholar were penetrated by a sense of the realness, more the sacredness, of the natural as well as the supernatural order; as something which was not to be fled from but to be loved without possessiveness, with an unlimited and humble tenderness, cleansed of all desire."[3] She goes on to quote one of von Hügel's greatest and most characteristic sayings, "God is a stupendously rich Reality; he is the God of nature, as well as the God of supernature," and she adds, "St. Francis would have understood and welcomed that. Every movement of his life declares its truth."[4]

In another essay, devoted directly to the teaching of von Hügel, Evelyn Underhill refers to the projected title of his Gifford Lectures, which in fact were never completed, "The Reality of Finites and the Reality of God." Von Hügel detected a strong tendency in the Christianity of recent centuries, Catholic and Protestant alike, to stress the reality of God in opposition to the reality of this finite, historical world; a tendency to make much of the doctrine of redemption to the exclusion of the doctrine of creation. But any full human and Christian life demands both. "In all his teaching about life, the Baron never forgot the truth, that sanity and lowliness require our reverent acceptance of both levels of our mixed experience; not an arrogant choice between them. By a succession of images . . . he struggled to convey this steady vision of a graded world: the need of nature and grace, sense and spirit, 'the seen and unseen, the Good and the Better or Best'—held together not set in opposition—for the maturing of man's spirit and the full living out of his peculiar call. 'A polarity, a tension, a friction, a one thing at work in distinctly another thing'—this was for him a fundamental and inevitable character of our spiritual life."[5] We begin to see the force of two more of the sayings which the Baron recorded from Huvelin's counsel. "There is no deeper or more dangerous enemy for Christianity than anything which reduces it or makes it narrow" and "For you, the spirit to follow, is a spirit of blessing all creation."[6]

We touch here on a point which brings out a striking likeness with one of the principal themes of the school of Russian religious thinkers of the last hundred years. Through all the diversity of view to be found in Solovyov and Fyodorov, in Berdyaev and Bulgakov, in Florensky and Frank, one theme which is constant is the desire to do battle against antireligious humanism on the one side and antihumanist religion on the other. God's glory, they maintain, is not truly expounded in systems of thought which denigrate man. In introducing the thought of Solovyov for instance, Frank writes of "the indissoluble bond between faith in Jesus Christ as God, and faith in man. The greatness and holiness of God is *ipso facto* the greatness and holiness—indeed, potential divinity—of his creature man and of all the world."[7] In all these writers we find, as in von Hügel, an attempt to do justice to the richly human implications of the Church's traditional faith in the incarnation.

Here is a vision of Christian life which insists on the claims both of nature and grace. It is a religion which encourages us to love God in all things *and* beyond all things, and which knows that we shall never be able to do either properly unless we are aiming in some measure to do both. We shall not truly find God in this world unless we are willing to turn away from it, to seek him in and for himself alone. But we shall never truly find God beyond this world unless we recognize that he is coming to us and making himself known in and through its most prosaic and earthly circumstances. In contemporary terms, we might say that the horizontal and vertical dimensions of Christian experience are inseparable and essential to one another. There is and there must be both a going out to others and a returning in to oneself, a movement of turning away from the world to God, and of rediscovering the world in God.

The inclusiveness of such a vision is a costly, not an easy thing. Evelyn Underhill sees it in the life of St. Francis in relation to two crucial events: the calling heard in prayer before the crucifix at San Damiano, and the mystery of La Verna. "His whole career, as I see it, is poised on these two strange events. The first drew him out towards the visible world, to help men and serve it. The second made him the mysterious partner of an invisible, rescuing love." Whenever we get him really speaking his mind, he is never far from the cross—the underlying tension of his life. " 'Yes, there it is; no need to go further,' " said Huvelin. " 'Sanctity and suffering are the same thing. You will do no good to others save in suffering and through suffering.' We draw very near the real Francis, though not near the popular notion of Francis, when we meditate on these words."[8] In words of considerable power she goes on to speak further of this the essential core of Francis' holiness. "The entire growth of Francis was towards the point at which, as that strange phrase in his legend says, he was 'transformed by the kindling of his mind into the image of the Crucified,' embracing and harmonising in one movement of self-abandoned love, the splendour of God and the deep suffering of man." That is Charity, the out-pouring passion of generous love at its full height, breadth and width; a passion which is the essence of eternal life, and reflects back to a metaphysical source. St. Francis, says the *Fioretti* in a famous passage, offered his followers "the chalice of life"; and those who had the courage to drink it, "saw in profound contemplation the abyss of the infinite divine light," a strange phrase for the sort of gift which the St. Francis of popular sentiment . . . is supposed to have made the world."[9] Here is a vision of St. Francis which rightly sees that grace and nature, joy and suffering, cross and resurrection must come together into one, if ever we are to understand the profound unity and wholeness, the liberating power of life.

Already we can begin to perceive something of the attraction of St. Francis for a theologian like Charles Raven, who was trying to make his fellow Christians recognize the proper claims of the natural sciences, the necessary place of the doctrine of creation in Christian life. Again in the refusal to say either God *or* men, either this world *or* the world to come which characterizes the saint, we can see the reason for a deep affinity between von Hügel and the Russian religious thinkers of whom we have already spoken. More specifically in the way in which cross and resurrection are held together, and man's turning toward God is seen as implying the raising up and not the abandonment of the creation, we recognize close parallels with the renewed patristic theology, which has been worked out by many Orthodox writers in the last thirty or forty years.

Fr. Dumitru Staniloae, one of the outstanding spokesmen of the Orthodox tradition in our time, writes of the significance of the cross, which is implanted on God's gift of the world to us and which becomes the way in which we are enabled to go beyond the gift to the giver. He cites the words of St. Maximus the Confessor, "all the realities which we perceive with the senses demand the cross," and "all the realities which we understand with our mind have need of the tomb," in order to stress that it is through death and burial that they may come to resurrection. And he himself writes, "The world has value only insofar as by it we see and receive the revelations and the energies of the person of God, who in himself in his essence, cannot be described, but whose energies are already at work in all creation and will be fully revealed in the transfigured world of the age to come . . . In the cross of Christ the salvation of the world is founded, the salvation of the whole cosmos, because by the cross the tendency of the whole cosmos to transcend itself into God is accomplished."[10]

This cosmic significance of the work of Christ and in particular of his death and resurrection is also emphasized by Vladimir Lossky in *The Mystical Theology of the Eastern Church* where, summing up the thought of St. Maximus, he says, "Man is not a being isolated from the rest of creation; by his very nature he is bound up with the whole of the universe, and St. Paul bears witness that 'the whole creation awaits the future glory which will be revealed in the sons of God.'[11] This cosmic awareness has never been absent from Eastern spirituality, and is given expression in theology as well as in liturgical poetry, in iconography and, perhaps, above all in the ascetical writings of the masters of the spiritual life of the Eastern Church . . . In his way to union with God, man in no way leaves aside but gathers together in his love the whole cosmos disordered by sin that it may at last be transfigured by grace."[12] In both these writers we find a note which is profoundly Franciscan.

And then we begin to notice other things in the Franciscan sources which make us want to reflect more deeply on the relation between St. Francis and the patristic tradition, Greek as well as Latin, which lay behind him. Details may catch our attention. For instance, we may notice the phrase already quoted from the *Fioretti* about "the abyss of the infinite divine light," and may recall how central a place the theme of "the uncreated light" has in the spirituality of the Eastern Church. Or again there are the remarks made by St. Francis when he compares a righteous man to an icon. "In pictures of God and the blessed Virgin painted on wood, God and the Blessed Virgin are held in mind, yet the wood and the painting ascribe nothing to themselves, because they are just wood and paint; so the servant of God is a kind of painting, that is a creature of God in which God is honoured for the sake of his benefits. But he ought to ascribe nothing to himself, just like the wood or the painting, but should render honour and glory to God alone . . ."[13] The person to whom such a comparison naturally suggested itself was evidently well acquainted with the theology which lies behind the veneration of icons in the Orthodox Church (that the honor paid to the icon passes to the one whom the icon portrays). It seems that he must also have been familiar with the actual making of icons, paintings on wood which are deliberately created so as to be vehicles and focal points of prayer.

This question about icons is perhaps more crucial and central than it might at first appear. In the flowering of art which followed on the period of St. Francis, that particular iconic understanding of the nature of religious painting was very soon lost. There is a quality about some of the very earliest representations of St. Francis and St. Clare, a transparent symbolic quality, which shows that they stand clearly within the iconographical tradition of the undivided Church. This is a quality which the later paintings, however beautiful in their own right, fail to convey. They become aesthetic works to be admired, not sacramental objects through which the saints approach us, and we are able to draw near to them. In icons the use of reversed perspective projects the figures toward us. The fact that the saints are always depicted frontally, their eyes looking straight at us, draws us into relationship with them. In this way the icon, like a sacrament, becomes a place of meeting between time and eternity, between man and God. In the case of the paintings of the Italian Renaissance, however, we have become spectators of a scene in which we are no longer directly involved; spectators, to be moved, uplifted maybe, by the devotional quality of the scene portrayed but no longer participants. It is all the difference between the liturgical use of Pauline material on the one side, "As many as have been baptised into Christ, have put on Christ," as in the idiom of Byzantine hymnography, and on the other side "When I survey the wondrous Cross." The fact that the latter piece is a very fine hymn no more destroys the difference than the fact that many of the paintings of the Italian Renaissance are very fine religious pictures. The gulf between them is nonetheless clear.

We move here in a very delicate area. For it is evident that hymns much less suitable than Isaac Watts' verses can and do function as real means of grace to believers who know no other tradition of worship, just as one observes that in many Orthodox Churches, icons which defy all the principles of correct iconography still function as icons. To discern that such pieces are objectively unsatisfactory does not mean that they are at once to be dismissed. But to recognize that the divine grace is at work through unsatisfactory media does not dispense us from the need to search for a true and more transparent image. Rather it suggests the need for certain criteria for future growth and development. There may indeed be a place for hymns and pictures of a reflective kind which look at the mysteries and ponder on them from a distance. But they should never displace the liturgical texts and objects which speak directly of the taking flesh of the Word of God and draw the worshiper into an immediate contact with the mysteries which they reveal.

An earlier generation of Western critics, which had not yet perceived either the significance or the creativity of later Byzantine art, would have said that in this period while the West progressed the East simply stagnated. But more recently it has become clear that this was not the case. The parallel yet different developments in Byzantine and Italian art in the thirteenth and fourteenth centuries have been noticed by many writers. There was a Renaissance in both parts of the Christian world, but whereas the growing humanism of the West more and more deprived religious painting of its theological and spiritual content, in the last centuries of the Eastern Christian Empire exactly the reverse seems to have happened. Patrick Leigh Fermor, for instance, a man with no theological axe to grind, remarks on this particular quality in late Byzantine painting, "As though by magic it humanized gods, angels, saints and mortals without draining them of a flicker of their spirituality . . . It is a miracle of delicate balance," which moves the viewer as well as exalting him.[14]

In the painting of an icon, the miracle of delicate balance of holding together natural and supernatural, seen and unseen, creation and redemption is particularly vital. It involves, in von Hügel's words, "a one thing at work in distinctly another thing." It is small wonder that in the Byzantine East at this period the miracle should rather frequently occur, for the theology and the spirituality of that time meditated long and deeply on the place of the body in man's spiritual development, and on the nature of the light revealed on Tabor in the face of Jesus Christ.

This theme finds its fullest expression in the writings of St. Gregory Palamas. But it is no less central in the work of his contemporary, Nicholas Cabasilas. Cabasilas was a layman, working in the imperial administration, a member of a circle of scholars and thinkers closely linked with the Italy of the Renaissance. In his writing, he consciously seeks to meet the growing attraction of the humanism of the West with another vision of the glory of man. As Panayiotis Nellas rightly points out, this is a vision of man which is strongly Christocentric, which underlines the necessity of man's renouncing his blind self-centred life if he is to find the only true life which can be his, a life centered upon God. So in the writings of the scholarly layman a strong ascetic and eschatological note is present. We see something of the way in which the monastic renunciations are discovered to be ways forward into the fullness of life and love in God. And he constantly insists that it is really man's nature which is transformed and renewed in the coming of God's grace. There is in the writings of Cabasilas a particular combination of the human and the divine, a vision both of the power and tenderness of God's love which is strangely Franciscan. In the writings of the scholar, as in the life of the saint, the creation is seen transfigured in the light which comes from the triumph of the cross.[15] In the West, however, after the time of St. Francis, this balance seems more and more to have been upset through the growth of a form of humanism which lost the vision of the transfiguration of the flesh. At a certain purely aesthetic level the works of the painters of the Umbrian School are triumphs of human creativity. But they have ceased to be windows opening onto the world of heavenly realities. We have only to place them beside the frescoes at Mistra or the icons of Rublev to perceive at once how much has been lost.

Do we have here a clue to the understanding of St. Francis? Is it, maybe, that to understand him more fully we need to see him against the background of the centuries which went before him, and of those which followed after in the Christian East, rather than against the more familiar story of the Medieval and Reformation West? It is difficult to avoid the feeling that despite all the wealth of devotion which his example evoked, his heritage became in some way divided, imperiled and obscured. In the remark of the Abbé Huvelin, which was quoted at the beginning of this article, the elipses, which indicate the omission of a phrase, stand for the rather cruel words "I do not say Franciscans." Doubtless the Abbé would not have wished to make too absolute a contrast between the saint and his followers, but reading the pages of Doctor Moorman's great history of the Franciscan Order one is forced at times to feel that there was something in the whole development of the thought and life of the Western Church in the later Middle Ages which fought against the full comprehension of the message of the saint. The growing legalism of the Latin tradition, the rationalism of much scholastic theology, the tendency to set one thing over against another, all made it increasingly difficult to live by the inclusiveness of the original vision. The theology of a Maximus the Confessor, which would provide a way of holding together the different facets of the saint's character, his love for all creation, his devotion to the cross, his joy in the resurrection would enable us to see more deeply the unity and wholeness of that amazing life, "Embracing and harmonising in one movement of self-abandoned love, the splendour of God and the deep suffering of man." But such a theology was scarcely to be found.

There is undoubtedly always a problem in the assimilation of the vision of a great and outstanding person by a very large number of his followers. The very popularity of St. Francis, his power of attracting men of very different kinds, has made this problem particularly acute in the case of the Franciscan Order. But there seems to be something more than this in the history of the fourteenth and fifteenth centuries. It is not just the tension between the spontaneity and inclusiveness of the origins and the necessary regularity and definition of the institution which grows out of them. A great part of the creativity of Francis' life and example grew out of the way in which it embodies a synthesis of opposites. "A polarity, a tension, a friction, a one thing at work in distinctly another thing," to recall von Hügel's words. He wanted his brethren to be at once contemplatives and apostles; to lead a life of solitude in hermitages and to lead a life of fraternity among men. He who sensed so sharply the beauty and richness of creation held out before his disciples the ideal of a most absolute poverty. He who was so full of joy at the knowledge of God's goodness, revealed alike in creation and redemption, was consumed with grief at his perception of the pain and sorrow of the cross. It was by way of the death on the cross that life and joy had come into the whole world.

All these polarities, which lie very close to the heart of the gospel, can be held together in a framework which acknowledges that life is larger either than law or logic, and which, while it despises neither man's rational nor his legal capacities, recognizes their limitations when we come to deal with the things of God. The way in which, in the later medieval Church, legal categories become more and more determinative within the church's structure, and administration made it increasingly difficult for the Franciscans to hold together the different aspects of the original vision in a living synthesis. The development of an increasingly rationalized theology had even deeper effects. Before the time of St. Francis, in East and West alike, theology had been a primarily monastic activity, a reflection on the mysteries of God growing directly out of a life of prayer and contemplation. Such a theology of experience has frequently to face the antimonies and paradoxes through which man's mind is led on its way toward God. In the centuries which followed, partly on account of the success of the Franciscans themselves, theology became an increasingly academic activity, pursued in the new and rapidly expanding universities of Western Europe. The requirements of human reason, of debate and dialectic, became more and more determinative of the shape of theological reflection. The coherent relationships between theology, liturgy and spirituality, which had characterized the earlier centuries, was increasingly broken. At the very heart of the Christian faith the unities of death and resurrection, of creation and redemption, of God and man were somehow threatened. God and man were seen in isolation, interpreted more and more exclusively in categories of a legal kind. The way was being prepared for the divisions and dichotomies of the sixteenth and seventeenth centuries. Only in our own century have Christians everywhere been led to reflect on ways in which a living synthesis may be discovered anew.

In this process of rediscovery it is clear that St. Francis has an important part. The attraction which he has for Protestants is such a massive phenomenon of the church history of this century as to need no underlining. There is however room for further reflection on its meaning. As to the attraction of St. Francis for the Christian East, that also is beginning to become evident. In this article we have attempted to explore some of the reasons for it. We have suggested that the tradition of the Eastern Church, with its consistently cosmic vision of the work of Christ and the Spirit, its refusal to separate the theology of the cross from the theology of glory, its deep conviction that the sacrament of the altar is inseparable from the sacrament of our brother, has much to teach us, not least in coming to understand the things which we have received from him. The intuition that we need to hold together in one aspect of faith and life which too often become opposed to one another, which was so characteristic of the thought of von Hügel, finds in the Orthodox tradition a powerful confirmation. It is exemplified incomparably in the life of St. Francis. In all the diversity of their ways, the Baron and the Poor Man both alike bear witness to that "stupendously rich Reality" which is God. Both alike liberate within us the possibility of sharing more deeply in that reconciling, unifying work which is brought about by the creative and redeeming power of grace.

Anglicans who have long attempted in their church life to hold together tendencies and persons apparently irreconcilable may feel that they have some particular contribution to make here; some insight and experience which may be more widely useful, particularly in the Roman Catholic Church in these years following Vatican II. I believe that we may indeed have something to offer, but only on condition that we offer it in fear and trembling, not supposing that we have already succeeded in effecting a synthesis and making a reconciliation, but knowing always that this fullness has been for our Church an aim, a goal which we have never achieved, and which, indeed, we could not achieve except in union with all our Christian brethren.

The Reconciliation of Opposites

1. F. von Hügel, *Selected Letters 1896–1924*, edited with a Memoir by Bernard Holland (London, 1927), p. 60.
2. Evelyn Underhill, *Mixed Pasture*, Twelve *Essays and Addresses* (London, 1933), p. 156.
3. *Ibid.*, p. 156.
4. *Ibid.*, p. 157.
5. *Ibid.*, p. 213.
6. *Op. cit.*, pp. 61, 62.
7. S. L. Frank, Introduction to *A Solovyov Anthology* (London, 1950).
8. *Op. cit.*, p. 161.
9. *Ibid.*, pp. 161–62.
10. Fr. Dumitru Staniloae, "The Cross on the Gift of the World," *Sobornost* Series 6: No. 2. (1971), p. 110.
11. Romans 8: 18–22.
12. V. Lossky, *The Mystical Theology of the Eastern Church* (1957), pp. 110–11.
13. *Scripta Leonis, Rufini et Angeli*, ed. R. B. Brooke (Oxford, 1970), p. 273.
14. Patrick Leigh Femor, *Mani, Travels in the Southern Peloponnese* (London, 1958) p. 229.
15. *Cf.* P. Nellas, *Introduction to the Study of Nicholas Cabasilas* (Athens, 1968), in Greek.
16. Part of the material of this essay was first published as an article in *The Franciscan*, Vol. XVII, No. 4 (September, 1975). I am grateful to Dr. D. G. Koutroubis of Athens and to Fr. Ignatius Kelly, O.F.M. of the Franciscan Study Centre in Canterbury for their helpful comments which encouraged me to rewrite and expand what I had originally written.

List of Contributors

Arthur Macdonald Allchin is a Canon Residentary of Canterbury Cathedral and Warden of the Community of the Sisters of the Love of God in Oxford. He was earlier Librarian at Pusey House, and sometime Lecturer at the General Theological Seminary in New York.

Horace W. B. Donegan is the Twelfth Bishop of New York, retired in 1972. He is presently on the staff of St. James Church, Madison Avenue, New York, of which he was Rector before being elected to the episcopate.

Reginald H. Fuller was Professor of New Testament at Union Theological Seminary in New York before joining the faculty of Virginia Theological Seminary in 1972.

William B. Green is Professor of Systematic Theology at the Episcopal Seminary in Austin, Texas, and a former Chaplain and Associate Professor of Religion at Vassar College.

Alan W. Jones is Associate Professor of Ascetical Theology at the General Theological Seminary in New York and the Founder and Director of the Center for Christian Spirituality. He was former Assistant Director of

Trinity Institute and Chaplain of St. Hilda's and St. Hugh's Schools.

Leslie J. A. Lang is retired Rector of St. Peter's, Westchester, New York and a trustee of St. Hilda's and St. Hugh's Schools and the General Theological Seminary.

Madeleine L'Engle is a poet and novelist and librarian at the Cathedral Church of St. John the Divine. She has received the Newberry Prize, the Sequoia Award and Austrian State Prize.

John Macquarrie is a Canon of Christ Church and Lady Margaret Professor of Divinity at Oxford University. He was formerly professor at Union Seminary in New York.

The authors wish to acknowledge and honor Mr. David Pizarro, Organist and Master of Choirsters at the Cathedral Church of St. John the Divine, whose original anthem, the text of which is based on the twenty-first chapter of *Revelation*, was written in honor of Canon West and was first performed on June 6, 1976 at the Cathedral.